D0285192

THE BALTI COOKBOOK

First published in Great Britain in 1996 by Hamlyn
an imprint of Reed Consumer Books Limited
Michelin House, 81 Fulham Road,
London SW3 6RB
and Auckland, Melbourne, Singapore and Toronto

ISBN 0 600 589 412

A CIP catalogue record for this book is available from the British Library.

Printed in the United Kingdom.

Notes

Both metric and imperial measurements have been given in all recipes.
Use one set of measurements only and not a mixture of both.
Standard level spoon measurements are used in all recipes.
1 tablespoon = one 15 ml spoon
1 teaspoon = one 5 ml spoon
Eggs should be size 3 unless otherwise stated.
Milk should be full fat unless otherwise stated.
Pepper should be freshly ground black pepper unless otherwise stated.
Fresh herbs should be used unless otherwise stated. If unavailable use dried herbs as an alternative but halve the quantities stated.
Ovens should be preheated to the specified temperature – if using a fan assisted oven, follow the manufacturer's instructions for adjusting the time and temperature.
To test if poultry is cooked, pierce the flesh through the thickest part with a skewer or fork – the juices should run clear, never pink or red.
Do not re-freeze poultry which has been previously frozen and thawed.
Do not re-freeze a cooked dish which has been previously frozen and thawed.

Acknowledgements

Art Director Keith Martin
Art Editor Mark Winwood
Designer Margaret Sadler
Commisioning Editor Nicky Hill
Editors Maggie Ramsay
Kathy Steer
Production Controller Melanie Frantz
Illustrator Colin Hadley

Contents

Introduction

The deepest roots of Balti cooking lie in the remote, almost inaccessible region of Baltistan, in northern Pakistan, but to find authentic Balti cooking as we know it today you need travel no further than the heart of England – the part of Birmingham that is sometimes known as 'Little Pakistan', or the 'Balti Belt'.

No one claims a long history for the Balti craze that has swept across Britain. It started in the eastern suburbs of Birmingham in the early 1970s, and is still happily evolving. This is a new cuisine, waiting for you to give it your individual touch, as do all the best Balti cooks. We hope this book will give you the confidence to cook Balti-style whenever you like.

What is Balti?

Balti describes the place of distant origin (Baltistan, northern Pakistan), the cooking pot (Balti pan, also known as a karhai, and very similar to a wok), and the delicious, subtly spicy food cooked in it.

The Himalayas separate China from Baltistan, so it is not surprising that a wok-like cooking pan should have appeared there. Today's Balti curries are usually stir-fried, although in restaurants the last-minute stir-frying is often an assembly of a spicy sauce with marinated or pre-cooked meat. Balti food may be quite dry, or have a rich sauce or 'gravy'; it differs from other curries in its shorter cooking time, which means that the flavours of the individual ingredients remain distinct. As a general rule, Balti food does not use an abundance of chillies; chillies are used with discretion, for their own flavour, rather than simply to make a searingly hot curry.

The original 1970s Baltis had a base of onion, tomato and herbs and spices such as coriander, fenugreek (methi) and cumin, but today anything goes.

A Brief History

Although the Balti phenomenon is new, it can be enlightening to understand its evolution, beginning well over a thousand years ago with nomadic tribespeople in the cold Himalayan region, who needed to keep culinary equipment to a minimum and therefore chose a versatile wok-like pan, which could be used for braising, boiling and frying.

After the partition of India in 1947, many Muslims from the newly created Pakistan left their native land to settle in distant cities. At the time there was plenty of work in Birmingham, and many Pakistanis found houses in the city's eastern suburbs. Their cafés were basic in menu and decor, and existed mainly to sell snacks and sweets to Asian customers. The food was drawn from the old cuisine of northern Pakistan, which itself had been influenced by China and Tibet, the spices of neighbouring Kashmir, and the richer tastes of the Mogul emperors. In Birmingham it was adapted to local availability of ingredients and the demand for something quick to eat. Most family cooking was done in the home, and there were few such public eating places until the 1970s.

By this time, Indian restaurants had become popular throughout Britain; their clientele was predominantly non-Asian and they had a wide appeal because the food was such good value. However, at its most basic level, the standard Indian repertoire consisted of curry – meat or chicken, hot, hotter or hottest – with rice. The discovery, in eastern Birmingham in the early 1970s, of a different sort of Indian food, where the spicing was subtle and every ingredient could be tasted, was a revelation. This type of cooking was described as Balti, and was served sizzling hot from the pan. The restaurant that produced this type of food became known as a Baltihouse.

Word soon spread, and enterprising Baltihouse owners began to introduce elements from the more widely known Indian menu, which itself was becoming more varied and subtle. The Baltihouses remained informal, inexpensive places, mainly unlicensed because of the adherence to the Muslim ban on alcohol, although customers could bring their own beer or wine.

Balti today is fast food, Indian style. In the 80 or so established Baltihouses there is a great element of fun. The idea of mixing and matching borrowed from pizzerias means that anything goes, to the extent that chicken, prawns and lamb are often served together, and Balti Mt-Spi-Mush can be deciphered as meat, spinach and mushroom.

Several Balti cookbooks have been written from the point of view of recreating dishes from restaurants. While this is fun to do, it has its drawbacks. Perhaps most importantly, chefs work on a much larger scale than everyday home cooks. While it is possible to adapt the techniques of the restaurant chef – after all, spices can be stored in a cool, dark, dry, airtight container, spice pastes and sauces in the refrigerator – we have created this book for the home cook. Each recipe is self-contained, and all the information you need to make it appears on the page.

The Balti Menu

A selection of appetizers is found in most Baltihouses, sometimes in a cold cabinet, so you can choose your own. As the food can be served very quickly, customers may decide to go without a first course, but at the very least there may be a yogurt and mint dip and poppadums to nibble while you wait.

Ancient Baltistani cuisine was probably based on a large amount of game: wild goat, venison, quail, partridge and pheasant, with mutton from the flocks of sheep kept by the tribesmen. The mountainous area was not hospitable to cattle, so beef was not on the menu. Neither was pork, because of the Muslim faith of the Baltistanis. Fish from the sea was out of the question, but freshwater fish and shellfish were plentiful, although not particularly popular. It is generally believed that the original Pakistani Balti dishes were quite dry, whereas today's recipes often include a thickish sauce or gravy.

In Birmingham, Balti chefs proved very adaptable, making use of the ingredients available in markets. Recently they have shamelessly borrowed ideas from established Indian restaurants. Many Balti dishes are inspired by standard fare such as Tandoori Chicken and Rogan Josh; they are no less authentic in the current Balti movement.

Balti dishes are usually served in a small karhai, with naan or other Indian bread. Many Asians do not use cutlery, preferring to eat with their fingers, and the original Baltihouse customers used pieces of bread to scoop food direct from the Balti pan.

Perhaps reflecting the fact that most Birmingham Baltihouses began as more of a snack-stop than a restaurant, many of them are also 'sweet centres', where very sweet, subtly spiced, often vividly coloured sweetmeats and puddings are kept chilled. We have included recipes for the most popular variations of the Indian ice cream known as Kulfi, syrupy Jallebi and fudge-like Barfi. Alternatively, serve fresh fruit such as mango, or an exotic fruit salad as a dessert.

Drinks

Most Baltihouses are unlicensed, since their owners are Muslims, and forbidden alcohol. However, British restaurant customers like to drink beer or wine with their meal, and so the custom of bringing their own developed. As an alternative to alcohol, the cool yogurt drink Lassi is a good accompaniment to all types of spicy food.

The Balti Pan

Some restaurants will tell you that Balti means 'bucket', and this may describe a pan of alternative shape to the one we know today: after all, a bucket shape would be very good to push down into the glowing embers of a fire for long, slow cooking. The large, shallow, rounded base of a wok would have been an improvement, reducing cooking time and heating the food more evenly.

Invented by the Chinese, the versatile wok was adopted throughout Asia, and can be used for almost any cooking technique, including braising, steaming and deep-frying. In India, where a similar pan is known as a karhai, it is used for deep-frying savoury Samosas and traditional sweets such as Jallebi.

In this book we have referred to the main cooking pot as a wok, since this is more familiar, but whether it is known as a Balti pan, karhai or wok, the wide, round-bottomed pan is ideal for all types of cooking. The double-handled pan is more stable for long simmering, while a single-handled wok makes stir-frying easier. A large deep frying pan can be used as an alternative.

The karhai – sometimes spelt karihai or kadhai – or Balti pan comes in every size from a huge 90 cm (3 feet) to a tiny 7.5 cm (3 inch) diameter; in a restaurant, each has its purpose. At home, a standard wok with a diameter of about 35 cm (14 inches) will cook food for 4–6 people. To make a chicken or meat dish and a vegetable accompaniment you would ideally need two woks, although a wok and a large frying pan will do. The traditional karhai is made from various metals and alloys, the most common of which are iron, aluminium and stainless steel.

If you join the swelling ranks of Balti addicts, you may like to invest in a few Balti serving dishes. These are smaller versions of the cooking pot, about 12 cm (5 inches) in diameter, and come with a wooden base, which is essential, as you will see. To achieve the sensational sizzling effect seen and heard in Indian restaurants you need to place a dry Balti serving dish over a very hot burner on the stove for around 5 minutes. When the dish is very hot, turn off the heat and add 1 teaspoon of oil or ghee, then stand back and add a few drops of water. Very carefully place the hot dish on a wooden stand, then add the hot food and serve at once. Warn your guests not to touch the hot metal dish.

Seasoning the Balti Pan

As with a wok, you can make a Balti pan practically nonstick by seasoning it before use. If it has been stored for a long time it will probably need seasoning again.

Scrub the pan to remove any grease or rust. Rinse and dry well. Put 4 tablespoons of oil in the pan and place over a medium heat. Leave it there until the oil begins to smoke, then remove from the heat and swirl the oil around the sides of the pan. Cool; then pour away the oil. Rub the pan with wads of kitchen paper until the paper comes away clean.

Ghee and Oil

The nomadic Baltistanis would probably have cooked with a type of ghee or clarified butter, an easily transportable fat that was more readily available than any oil, and prepared in such a way as to make it keep for a long time. You can make your own ghee (see recipe, page 11) or buy it from many supermarkets or Asian shops. Vegetable oil is a healthier alternative, and either can be used. We have suggested ghee for recipes with a richer-tasting result, and vegetable oil for others. Any vegetable oil can be used, although the powerful flavours of olive oil do not combine well with these spicy dishes. Some recipes are derived from southern Indian specialities, and use mustard oil: this is sold in Asian shops or some supermarkets, or can be replaced with another oil.

Fish, Poultry and Meat

All types of fish and shellfish are perfect for the quick, stir-fried Balti technique, so use whatever is available at your fishmonger or supermarket.

Poultry is always skinned for use in Balti cooking. Although it cooks quickly, always take out a piece when the cooking time is up and check that it is properly cooked through by piercing it with a skewer and the juices runing clear.

In Balti restaurants, meat is par-cooked, by simmering it with spices, so it can be quickly stir-fried. At home, you can use lean, tender lamb such as leg steaks or neck fillet, which does not need pre-cooking.

Herbs and Spices

Asafoetida – Light brown resin, often sold = ground to a powder. It has a strong smell, a distinctive flavour and is used in bean and lentil dishes.

Ajowan (Lovage Seeds) – Greenish brown seeds with a strong aroma, popular in Indian cooking. If unavailable, thyme leaves are a good substitute.

Cardamom (Elaichi) – Three types of pods: brown, green and white. The green and white pods are small with a delicate aromatic flavour while the brown ones are much larger and are slightly more pungent.
Chillies – Fresh chillies can be green or red, large or small. Dried whole red chillies are very hot especially the smaller ones. Chilli powder is made from ground dried red chillies. The heat and flavour of fresh, dried and ground chillies varies enormously, so always add small amounts first, taste and adjust the amount as required.
Warning: Always take care when using fresh chillies. After preparation, wash your hands, knives and chopping board thoroughly and never let any part of the chilli go near your eyes or nose.
Cinnamon – This spice has an aromatic and sweet flavour. Sold in powder and in sticks.
Coconut – While not authentic to Balti cooking, it is popular because of its richness and delicious flavour. When buying fresh coconut, choose one which sounds as if it has plenty of liquid inside. Drain the liquid by making holes in 2 of the 3 'eyes' then cook for 15 minutes in a preheated oven, 160°C (325°F), Gas Mark 3. Crack open and scoop out the flesh, then grind in a food processor. Alternatives are desiccated coconut or coconut powder. The latter is finely ground coconut flesh which, when mixed with milk or water becomes a creamy paste. Creamed coconut, sold in blocks, must be chopped coarsely and melted in a liquid base. Canned coconut milk is good for making sauces.
Coriander (Dhania) – Fresh coriander leaves give a distinctive fragrant taste when added towards the end of cooking time or as a garnish. The greyish brown seeds have a warm spicy flavour and are available whole or ground. Ground coriander loses its flavour if stored too long.
Cumin (Jeera) – The seeds are narrow and shaped like caraway seeds with a distinctive mildly hot flavour. Ground cumin is available in most supermarkets.
Curry leaves – Fresh or dried aromatic leaves which give a lemony taste to dishes.
Fennel seeds (Soonf) – Aniseed-flavoured seeds which are yellowy green and used in many Indian dishes.
Fenugreek (Methi) – Available fresh as a dark green leaf with a savoury taste and also as yellow seeds which have a savoury but bitter flavour. Both should be used with care.
Garam masala – A mixture of highly aromatic spices widely used in Balti dishes. It is best to make your own (see page 11) but can be bought ready-made from Asian shops and most supermarkets. Usually added towards the end of the cooking time.
Ginger – One of the most popular spices in Indian cooking. Fresh root ginger should be peeled before use then chopped, grated or puréed. Often used in Balti cooking.
Lemon grass – A long, slim citrus-flavoured bulb available from Asian shops and most supermarkets. Can be used whole (and removed before serving) or chopped. To chop, cut off the root tip, peel away the outer layers and then chop the inner layers finely.
Kalonji – (Black Onion Seeds or Nigella) Black irregular tiny nugget-shaped seeds which have a peppery flavour once cooked.
Mace – The lacy outer covering on the nutmeg kernel.

Mango powder (Amchoor) – Dried ground mangoes, which have a slightly sour flavour.
Mustard seeds (Rai) – These are small brown seeds and are quite hot.
Saffron (Zafran) – Deep orange stigma of a crocus, available in threads or as a powder. It gives a yellow colour and a subtle aroma and flavour.
Tamarind – Sour-tasting fruit resembling a long date. Often sold dried and compressed in blocks. To use, cut off part of the block, add it to 4 x its volume of water in a pan. Bring the water to simmering point. Cool and push the pulp through a sieve to give a thick liquid. Discard the pulp. Tamarind paste, sold in jars in Indian shops, is easier to use. If unavailable, use a little lemon juice or vinegar.
Turmeric – The ground root of the turmeric plant, gives dishes a distinctive yellow colour.
Shrimp paste – A southeast Asian ingredient, sold in a compressed block, with a strong smell. Although shrimp paste does not go off, make sure it is well cooked.

Techniques and Basic Recipes

Many spices can be bought already ground into powder, but a better flavour is obtained if you buy the whole seeds and grind them yourself. First you should dry-roast them (either in a small pan, under the grill, or in the oven at 160°C (325°F), Gas Mark 3) for a few minutes, just enough to bring out their fragrance. Do not let them burn. They can then be ground, either in a spice mill, blender or mortar.
All dried pulses and beans, except lentils and split peas, must be soaked before cooking. First, rinse them, then cover with 2–3 times their volume of cold water and leave for 10 hours, or overnight. After soaking, drain and rinse in fresh water. Put the pulses in a large pan and cover with water. Bring to the boil, lower the heat and simmer until tender. Follow the packet instructions on individual soaking and cooking times.
Ghee – To make 175 g/6 oz, melt 250 g/8 oz butter over a low heat. Leave to simmer for 45 minutes. It will separate into golden butter and whitish milk solids. Skim the top, then pour off the clarified butter and discard the milk solids left in the pan.

Garam masala – This is a basic recipe for garam masala
3 tablespoons coriander seeds
1½ tablespoons cumin seeds
3 x 5 cm/2 inch pieces of cinnamon stick
1 tablespoon fennel seeds
1 teaspoon whole cloves
1 teaspoon mace blades
1 teaspoon ground cardamom
1 teaspoon ground nutmeg
Dry-roast each of the spices separately in a frying pan until they are fragrant but not dark. As each spice is roasted tip into a bowl and cool. Place the spices in a blender or mortar and grind to a powder. Transfer the blended spices to a bowl and stir in the cardamom and nutmeg. Store in an airtight container in a cool dark place. It keeps for 2–3 months.

SOUPS AND STARTERS

THROUGHOUT THE INDIAN SUBCONTINENT THE DAY IS PUNCTUATED WITH SNACKS, OFTEN BOUGHT FROM STREET VENDORS AND TRADITIONALLY OFFERED TO GUESTS AS A SIGN OF WELCOME. IN THE BALTIHOUSES OF BRITAIN, THESE SNACKS HAVE BEEN ADOPTED INTO THE MENU AS FIRST COURSES, TAKING THEIR PLACE ALONGSIDE SOUPS AND OTHER APPETIZERS, MANY OF WHICH CAN BE PREPARED IN ADVANCE.

Spiced Chicken Soup

1.5 LITRES/2½ PINTS BOILING WATER
1.2 KG/2½ LB CHICKEN, QUARTERED
4 UNCOOKED LARGE PRAWNS, SHELLED AND DEVEINED, SHELLS RESERVED
2 MACADAMIA NUTS, CHOPPED
4 SHALLOTS, CHOPPED
2 GARLIC CLOVES, CHOPPED
2 TEASPOONS GRATED FRESH ROOT GINGER
A PINCH OF GROUND TURMERIC
A PINCH OF CHILLI POWDER
VEGETABLE OIL FOR SHALLOW FRYING
1 TABLESPOON LIGHT SOY SAUCE
ABOUT 75 G/3 OZ BEAN SPROUTS
SALT AND PEPPER
1 POTATO, SLICED VERY THINLY, TO GARNISH

Place 1.5 litres/2½ pints boiling water in a large saucepan, add the chicken, prawn shells and a little salt and pepper. Cover and simmer for 40 minutes. Strain and reserve 1.2 litres/2 pints of the liquid. Shred the meat from the chicken.

Purée the macadamias, shallots, garlic and ginger in a liquidizer, then add the turmeric and chilli powder and mix well.

Heat 2 tablespoons of the oil in a wok, add the spice paste and fry for a few seconds. Stir in 300 ml/½ pint of the reserved liquid, the soy sauce, chicken and prawns. Simmer for 5 minutes. Add the remaining cooking liquid and simmer for a further 5 minutes. Add the bean sprouts and cook for 3 minutes. Adjust the seasoning to taste. Meanwhile, fry the potato slices in hot oil until crisp. Serve the soup hot, garnished with the fried potato.

SERVES 4–6
PREPARATION TIME: 20 MINUTES
COOKING TIME: ABOUT 50 MINUTES

Fish Soup with Coconut

625 G/1¼ LB MONKFISH OR HALIBUT FILLET, SKINNED AND CUBED
25 G/1 OZ DESICCATED COCONUT
6 SHALLOTS
6 ALMONDS, BLANCHED
2–3 GARLIC CLOVES
2.5 CM/1 INCH PIECE FRESH ROOT GINGER, PEELED AND SLICED
2 STEMS LEMON GRASS, ROOTS TRIMMED
2–3 TEASPOONS GROUND TURMERIC
3 TABLESPOONS VEGETABLE OIL
400 ML/14 FL OZ COCONUT MILK
1–2 FRESH RED OR GREEN CHILLIES, DESEEDED AND SLICED
SALT
A FEW SPRIGS OF FRESH CORIANDER, TO GARNISH

Sprinkle the fish with salt. Place the coconut in a wok or heavy-based frying pan and heat until golden and crisp. Remove and pound until oily. Purée the shallots, almonds, garlic, ginger and 6 cm/2½ inches from the root end of the lemon grass (reserve the remainder) in a liquidizer. Add the turmeric.

Heat the oil and fry the puréed mixture for a few minutes. Add the coconut milk and bring to the boil, stirring constantly. Add the fish, chillies, and the remaining lemon grass and cook for 3–4 minutes. Stir in the pounded coconut and cook for 2–3 minutes. Remove the stems of lemon grass, transfer to a large serving bowl and garnish with sprigs of fresh coriander.

SERVES 4
PREPARATION TIME: 25 MINUTES
COOKING TIME: ABOUT 15 MINUTES

Mulligatawny Soup

- 50 G/2 OZ DRIED TAMARIND
- 1.2 LITRES/2 PINTS BEEF STOCK
- 50 G/2 OZ GHEE OR BUTTER (SEE PAGE 11)
- 1 LARGE ONION, SLICED
- 2 GARLIC CLOVES, SLICED
- 1 TEASPOON GROUND GINGER
- 2 TEASPOONS PEPPER
- 2 TEASPOONS GROUND CORIANDER
- ½ TEASPOON GROUND FENUGREEK
- ½ TEASPOON CHILLI POWDER
- ½ TEASPOON GROUND TURMERIC
- ½ TEASPOON SALT

Put the dried tamarind in a saucepan, add just enough of the beef stock to cover, then bring to the boil. Remove the pan from the heat, cover and leave the tamarind to soak for 4 hours.

Melt the ghee or butter in a wok or heavy-based saucepan, add the onion and garlic and fry gently until soft, about 4–5 minutes. Add the spices and salt and fry for 3 minutes, stirring constantly. Stir in the remaining beef stock. Strain the tamarind liquid through a wire sieve set over a small bowl, pressing to extract as much liquid as possible. Add the tamarind juice to the wok and simmer for 15 minutes. Taste and adjust the seasoning before serving. Serve hot.

SERVES 4

PREPARATION TIME: 10 MINUTES, PLUS 4 HOURS SOAKING

COOKING TIME: 25 MINUTES

Steamed Lentil Cakes

375 g/12 oz red lentils (masoor dal)
1 teaspoon ground cumin
1 teaspoon chilli powder
1 teaspoon salt
½ teaspoon pepper
25 g/1 oz fresh coriander leaves, chopped
juice of 1 lemon
250 g/8 oz natural yogurt

Wash the lentils thoroughly. Drain well, place in a large bowl and add 1.8 litres/3 pints cold water. Leave to soak for 36 hours.

Drain and discard the water and grind the lentils to a fine paste in a liquidizer or food processor. Using muslin or a strong tea towel, squeeze the excess water from the lentils. Transfer the paste to a bowl and mix in the cumin, chilli powder, salt, pepper and coriander. Shape into 6–8 cakes, 5 cm/2 inches in diameter and 1 cm/½ inch thick. Pat dry with kitchen paper.

Place the cakes in the top of a steamer, cover and then steam for 1 hour. If you do not have a steamer, place in a shallow dish and stand the dish in a roasting tin filled with enough hot water to come halfway up the sides of the dish. Cover with foil, then place in a preheated oven, 190°C (375°F), Gas Mark 5, and cook for 1 hour. When cooked, remove from the steamer or oven and leave to cool.

Mix the lemon juice into the yogurt. Put the lentil cakes in a shallow dish and cover with the yogurt mixture. Marinate in the refrigerator for at least 2 hours before serving.

Makes 6–8

Preparation time: 25 minutes, plus soaking and marinating

Cooking time: 1 hour

Vegetable Fritters

175 G/6 OZ PLAIN FLOUR OR CHICKPEA FLOUR (GRAM FLOUR OR BESAN)
½ TEASPOON SALT
½ TEASPOON BICARBONATE OF SODA
½ TEASPOONS GROUND CORIANDER
½ TEASPOON GROUND TURMERIC
¾ TEASPOON WHOLE AJOWAN SEEDS (OPTIONAL)
1 TEASPOON PEPPER
VEGETABLE OIL FOR DEEP-FRYING
1 POTATO, SLICED
1 SMALL CAULIFLOWER, BROKEN INTO FLORETS

Sift the flour with the salt and bicarbonate of soda into a mixing bowl. Add the spices, then slowly whisk in 300 ml/½ pint water, to make a smooth batter.

Heat the oil in a large wok to 180–190°C (350–375°F), or until a cube of bread browns in 30 seconds.

Dip the potato slices into the batter to coat thoroughly. Shake off any excess batter and deep-fry until golden brown and crisp. Remove with a slotted spoon and drain on kitchen paper.

Coat and fry the cauliflower in the same way. Serve the fritters hot, with tomato chutney.

SERVES 6–8
PREPARATION TIME: 20 MINUTES
COOKING TIME: ABOUT 20 MINUTES

Pakora

1 onion, chopped roughly
¼ lemon, chopped roughly
300 ml/½ pint natural yogurt
1 teaspoon chilli powder
½ teaspoon mustard powder
150–175 g/5–6 oz chickpea flour (gram flour or besan), sifted
vegetable oil for deep-frying

Filling:
1 aubergine, cut into 3 mm/⅛ inch slices
spinach leaves, washed and thoroughly dried

Place the onion, lemon and yogurt in a liquidizer and blend to a smooth sauce. Pour this into a large mixing bowl and add the chilli powder and mustard.

Gradually whisk in the flour until the batter forms small peaks which hold their shape for 15–20 seconds. Depending on how liquid the yogurt is, you may have to add more or less flour.

Heat the oil in a large wok to 180–190°C (350–375°F), or until a cube of bread browns in 30 seconds.

Dip the aubergine slices into the batter to coat thoroughly. Shake off the excess batter and deep-fry until they are golden brown and crisp. Remove with a slotted spoon and drain on kitchen paper. Coat and fry the spinach leaves in the same way. Serve hot.

Serves 4
Preparation time: 20 minutes
Cooking time: about 20 minutes

Sweet and Sour Potatoes

3 TABLESPOONS VEGETABLE OIL
1 TEASPOON BLACK MUSTARD SEEDS
1 TEASPOON CUMIN SEEDS
6 POTATOES, CUBED
2 TEASPOONS GROUND CORIANDER
1 TEASPOON GROUND TURMERIC
1 TEASPOON CHILLI POWDER
2 TEASPOONS SALT
4 TEASPOONS BROWN SUGAR
5 TABLESPOONS TOMATO PURÉE
3 TABLESPOONS VINEGAR
5–6 SPRIGS OF FRESH CORIANDER LEAVES, CHOPPED, TO GARNISH

Heat the oil in a wok or heavy-based frying pan, add the mustard and cumin seeds and fry for 15–20 seconds, until they pop. Lower the heat and carefully add the potatoes. Add the ground coriander, turmeric, chilli powder, salt, brown sugar, 300 ml/½ pint water, tomato purée and vinegar and stir well. Cover the wok and cook over a low heat until the potatoes are tender. Garnish with the chopped coriander and serve at once.

SERVES 4
PREPARATION TIME: 10–15 MINUTES
COOKING TIME: 25–30 MINUTES

Indian-style Scrambled Eggs

6 eggs
50 g/2 oz ghee or butter (see page 11)
1 onion, thinly sliced
1 garlic clove, thinly sliced
10 cm/4 inch piece fresh root ginger, peeled and cut into thin strips
1 teaspoon ground turmeric
1 teaspoon garam masala (see page 11)
½ teaspoon chilli powder
1 teaspoon salt
4 fresh green chillies, deseeded and chopped into 5 mm/¼ inch pieces
chopped fresh coriander leaves, to garnish

Whisk the eggs and reserve. Melt the ghee or butter in a wok, add the onion and garlic and fry for 4–5 minutes, until soft. Add the ginger and fry gently for 2 minutes more, stirring constantly.

Add the turmeric, garam masala, chilli powder and salt and cook gently for a further 1 minute, stirring constantly.

Whisk the eggs once again and add to the wok. Cook over a gentle heat, scraping the egg from the side of the wok until the mixture is soft and creamy. Remove from the heat immediately. It is important not to overcook the eggs.

Sprinkle the chopped chillies into the egg mixture, then fold gently to mix thoroughly. Pile the scrambled eggs on to slices of hot toast and sprinkle with chopped coriander leaves. Serve immediately.

Serves 4
Preparation time: 15 minutes
Cooking time: 15–20 minutes

Prawn and Egg Sambal

- 500 G/1 LB PEELED COOKED PRAWNS
- 4 HARD-BOILED EGGS, SHELLED AND QUARTERED
- 300 ML/½ PINT COCONUT MILK
- 1 SMALL ONION, FINELY CHOPPED
- 1 GARLIC CLOVE, CRUSHED
- 1 FRESH GREEN CHILLI, DESEEDED AND CHOPPED
- JUICE OF ½ LEMON
- A PINCH OF CHILLI POWDER
- ½ TEASPOON SALT

TO GARNISH:

- 50 G/2 OZ COOKED GREEN PEAS
- CHOPPED FRESH CORIANDER LEAVES

Arrange the prawns and eggs in a shallow serving dish, then chill them in the refrigerator.

Place the coconut milk, onion, garlic, chilli, lemon juice, chilli powder and salt in a liquidizer and purée until smooth and evenly mixed. Pour this mixture over the prawns and eggs. Garnish with the peas and chopped coriander.

Serve well chilled, with poppadoms if liked.

SERVES 4

PREPARATION TIME: 15 MINUTES, PLUS CHILLING

Prawn Croquettes

500 G/1 LB UNCOOKED PRAWNS, SHELLED AND DEVEINED
2 GARLIC CLOVES
1 HEAPED TABLESPOON CHOPPED FRESH ROOT GINGER
1 FRESH GREEN CHILLI
1 LARGE ONION, CHOPPED
½ TEASPOON GROUND TURMERIC
½ TEASPOON PEPPER
½ TEASPOON SALT
1 EGG, LIGHTLY BEATEN
FRESH WHITE BREADCRUMBS TO COAT
125 G/4 OZ GHEE OR BUTTER (SEE PAGE 11)

TO GARNISH:
COOKED PRAWNS IN THEIR SHELLS
SPRIGS OF FRESH MINT OR PARSLEY

Mince the prawns together with the garlic, ginger, chilli, onion, turmeric, pepper and salt. Use the finest blade on the mincer or alternatively use a liquidizer but be careful not to reduce the mixture to a liquid pulp.

Stir in the egg and form the mixture into 8 round croquettes approximately 5 cm/2 inches in diameter. Coat with the breadcrumbs, then chill in the refrigerator for 30 minutes.

Heat the ghee or butter in a large wok, then fry the croquettes until golden brown on all sides, turning once. This should take about 6–7 minutes.

Serve at once, garnished with whole prawns and a few sprigs of mint or parsley.

SERVES 4
PREPARATION TIME: 30 MINUTES, PLUS 30 MINUTES CHILLING
COOKING TIME: ABOUT 10 MINUTES

Tandoori King Prawns

300 ML/½ PINT NATURAL YOGURT
2 TABLESPOONS VINEGAR
1 TEASPOON SALT
1 TEASPOON PEPPER
½ TEASPOON PAPRIKA
½ TEASPOON CHILLI POWDER
1 TEASPOON GARAM MASALA (SEE PAGE 11)
1 TEASPOON GROUND FENUGREEK
RED FOOD COLOURING (OPTIONAL)
25 G/1 OZ FRESH ROOT GINGER, PEELED AND CHOPPED
12 WHOLE UNCOOKED LARGE PRAWNS
LEMON WEDGES, TO GARNISH

Prepare a marinade: put the yogurt and vinegar into a liquidizer with the salt, pepper, paprika, chilli powder, garam masala, fenugreek and ginger. Blend until a smooth sauce is obtained. Red colouring may be added, if liked. Set the marinade aside.

Prepare the prawns by cutting the heads off with a sharp knife. Pull off the legs and the shell, then remove the sand track which runs along the back, trying not to break the prawns up too much.

Pour the marinade over the shellfish, cover and marinate for about 2 hours in the refrigerator.

Thread the prawns on to metal skewers and grill or barbecue, turning once, until cooked – about 10 minutes. Serve immediately, garnished with lemon wedges.

SERVES 4
PREPARATION TIME: 15 MINUTES, PLUS 2 HOURS MARINATING
COOKING TIME: ABOUT 10 MINUTES

Vegetable Samosas

PASTRY:
125 G/4 OZ PLAIN FLOUR
¼ TEASPOON SALT
25 G/1 OZ GHEE OR BUTTER (SEE PAGE 11)
FILLING:
1 TABLESPOON VEGETABLE OIL
1 TEASPOON MUSTARD SEEDS
1 SMALL ONION, MINCED
2 GREEN CHILLIES, MINCED
¼ TEASPOON GROUND TURMERIC
1 TEASPOON FINELY CHOPPED FRESH ROOT GINGER
125 G/4 OZ FROZEN PEAS
125 G/4 OZ COOKED POTATOES, DICED
½ TABLESPOON CHOPPED CORIANDER
1 TABLESPOON LEMON JUICE
VEGETABLE OIL FOR DEEP-FRYING

Sift the flour and salt into a mixing bowl. Rub in the ghee or butter until the mixture resembles breadcrumbs. Add 2–3 tablespoons of cold water and knead lightly to form a smooth dough. Cover and chill in the refrigerator while preparing the filling.

Heat the oil in a saucepan and add the mustard seeds. Leave for a few seconds until they start to pop, then add the onion and fry until golden. Add the chillies, turmeric, ginger, salt to taste, and fry for about 3 minutes; if it starts sticking to the pan add ½ tablespoon of water and stir well. Add the peas, stir well and cook for 2 minutes. Add the potatoes and coriander, stir well and cook for 2 minutes. Stir in the lemon juice, then cool slightly.

Divide the pastry into 8 pieces. Dust with flour and roll each piece into a thin round, then cut each round in half. Fold each half into a cone, brush the edges lightly with water and pinch to seal. Fill the cone with a spoonful of filling (do not overfill), dampen the top edge and seal firmly. Deep-fry until crisp and golden. Serve warm.

SERVES 4
PREPARATION TIME: ABOUT 15–20 MINUTES
COOKING TIME: ABOUT 20 MINUTES

FISH AND SHELLFISH

THE IDEAL INGREDIENTS FOR BALTI COOKING, FISH AND SHELLFISH COOK VERY QUICKLY ONCE ADDED TO THE FRAGRANT, STIR-FRIED ONION AND SPICE BASE, AND THE FLAVOURS OF THE FISH COME THROUGH IN THE FINISHED DISH. DO NOT OVERCOOK FISH, OTHERWISE IT WILL BREAK UP INTO TINY FLAKES. ALMOST ANY FISH CAN BE COOKED BALTI-STYLE, BUT FIRM-TEXTURED WHITE FISH LIKE HALIBUT AND MONKFISH ARE EXCELLENT.

Balti Prawns

50 G/2 OZ GHEE OR BUTTER (SEE PAGE 11)
1 SMALL ONION, SLICED
2.5 CM.1 INCH PIECE FRESH ROOT GINGER, CHOPPED
2 GARLIC CLOVES, SLICED
2 TEASPOONS GROUND CORIANDER
½ TEASPOON GROUND GINGER
1 TEASPOON GROUND TURMERIC
½ TEASPOON GROUND CUMIN
½ TEASPOON CHILLI POWDER
2 TABLESPOONS VINEGAR
500 G/1 LB PEELED COOKED PRAWNS
1 RED OR GREEN PEPPER, DESEEDED AND CUT INTO SQUARES
1 TABLESPOON TOMATO PURÉE
CHOPPED FRESH CORIANDER LEAVES, TO GARNISH

Melt the ghee or butter in a large wok or heavy-based frying pan, add the onion and ginger and fry gently for 4–5 minutes, or until the onion is soft, then add the garlic.

Meanwhile, in a small bowl mix the coriander, ginger, turmeric, cumin and chilli powder to a paste with the vinegar, then add this paste to the wok and stir-fry for a further 3 minutes.

Add the cooked prawns with the pepper squares and turn gently with a wooden spoon until they are well coated with the spices. Add 200 ml/7 fl oz water with the tomato purée and stir well. Bring to the boil, simmer for 1–2 minutes then serve immediately, garnished with coriander leaves.

Serves 4
Preparation time: 10 minutes
Cooking time: 10–15 minutes

Balti Madras Prawns

50 G/2 OZ GHEE OR BUTTER
(SEE PAGE 11)
½ TEASPOON BLACK MUSTARD SEEDS
1 SMALL ONION, SLICED
2 GARLIC CLOVES, SLICED
1 TEASPOON GRATED FRESH ROOT GINGER
1 TEASPOON GROUND CORIANDER
½ TEASPOON CHILLI POWDER, PLUS EXTRA
TO GARNISH
½ TEASPOON GROUND TURMERIC
½ TEASPOON GROUND CUMIN
½ TEASPOON SALT
500 G/1 LB PEELED COOKED PRAWNS
1 TABLESPOON VINEGAR

Melt the ghee or butter in a large wok or heavy-based frying pan. When it is hot, add the mustard seeds and as soon as they begin to pop (5–10 seconds), add the onion and garlic and fry gently for about 4–5 minutes, until the onion is soft. Add the ginger, coriander, chilli powder, turmeric, cumin and salt and then stir-fry for 3 minutes more.

Lower the heat, then add the prawns and toss lightly for 1 minute or until the prawns are coated in the spices. Stir in the vinegar, increase the heat and cook for 30 seconds. Sprinkle with a little chilli powder and serve immediately.

SERVES 4
PREPARATION TIME: 5 MINUTES
COOKING TIME: ABOUT 10 MINUTES

Prawns with Tamarind

- 250 g/8 oz dried tamarind
- 1 small red pepper, deseeded and chopped
- 25 g/1 oz onion, chopped
- 2 garlic cloves, chopped
- 1 fresh red chilli, deseeded and chopped
- 1 tablespoon ground lemon grass
- 6 tablespoons vegetable oil
- 4 teaspoons caster sugar
- 2 teaspoons lime juice
- 500 g/1 lb uncooked large prawns in their shells, heads left on and deveined through the shells
- salt

First make the tamarind paste: place the dried tamarind and 125 ml/4 fl oz water in a small saucepan and bring to the boil. Cover and simmer for 10 minutes. Remove from the heat and leave to stand, covered, for 1 hour. Mash, then press the tamarind through a wire sieve set over a bowl. Reserve 3 tablespoons of the tamarind liquid and use the remainder for another dish.

Place the red pepper, onion, garlic, chilli and lemon grass in a liquidizer or food processor and blend. Heat the oil in a large wok, add the pepper mixture and stir-fry for 5 minutes. Gradually blend in the tamarind paste, sugar, lime juice and salt to taste. Add the prawns and stir-fry for 5 minutes, or until the prawns are just firm to the touch. Serve at once.

Serves 4

Preparation time: 10 minutes, plus 1 hour for the tamarind

Cooking time: about 10 minutes

Balti King Prawns with Tomatoes

500 G/1 LB UNCOOKED LARGE PRAWNS, SHELLED AND DEVEINED
50 G/2 OZ GHEE OR BUTTER (SEE PAGE 11)
3 ONIONS, CHOPPED
3 LARGE TOMATOES, SKINNED AND QUARTERED
¼ TEASPOON GARLIC POWDER
¼ TEASPOON GROUND GINGER
1 TEASPOON CHILLI POWDER
2 TEASPOONS GROUND CORIANDER
½ TEASPOON GROUND TURMERIC
2 TABLESPOONS DESICCATED COCONUT
2 TEASPOONS GARAM MASALA (SEE PAGE 11)
SALT

Sprinkle the prawns with salt. Heat the ghee or butter in a large wok and lightly fry the prawns until they just begin to turn pink. Remove and set aside.

Add the onions to the wok and stir-fry for 5–10 minutes, or until they are translucent and beginning to brown. Add the tomatoes and all the spices except the garam masala. Continue to cook for a further 5 minutes.

Return the prawns to the wok and stir-fry for 1–2 minutes, then add the coconut and 150 ml/¼ pint water and simmer until the prawns are almost cooked. Sprinkle on the garam masala and cook until the prawns are tender. Serve hot.

SERVES 4
PREPARATION TIME: 10 MINUTES
COOKING TIME: ABOUT 10–15 MINUTES

Prawn Pathia

75 g/3 oz ghee or butter (see page 11)
2 large onions, sliced
50 g/2 oz desiccated coconut
1 teaspoon chilli powder
2 teaspoons paprika
2.5 cm/1 inch piece cinnamon stick
2 bay leaves
1 teaspoon garam masala (see page 11)
2 teaspoons fenugreek seeds
25 g/1 oz fresh root ginger, peeled and chopped
125 g/4 oz tomato purée
300 ml/½ pint natural yogurt
500 g/1 lb uncooked prawns, shelled and deveined

Heat the ghee or butter in a large wok and fry the onions for about 5–10 minutes, or until they are golden brown.

Add the coconut and cook until golden brown, stirring frequently to make sure that none of it sticks to the bottom of the wok.

Stir in the chilli powder, paprika, cinnamon, bay leaves, garam masala, fenugreek, ginger, tomato purée and yogurt. Stir well and if necessary add a little hot water to make the sauce the consistency of thick yogurt.

When the mixture boils add the prawns immediately, turn down the heat, cover the wok and simmer very slowly until the prawns are cooked. Serve at once.

Serves 4
Preparation time: 20 minutes
Cooking time: about 20 minutes

Green Fenugreek Prawns

- 4 tablespoons vegetable oil
- 2 bunches spring onions, trimmed and sliced
- 3 fresh green chillies, finely sliced
- 2 garlic cloves, crushed
- 2.5 cm/1 inch piece fresh root ginger, peeled and grated
- 2 fresh green or red chillies, deseeded and chopped
- 1 teaspoon ground turmeric
- 500 g/1 lb peeled cooked prawns
- 1 teaspoon salt
- ½ bunch fresh fenugreek leaves, trimmed and chopped
- 4 tomatoes, sliced, to garnish

Heat the oil in a wok or heavy-based frying pan, add the spring onions and sliced chillies and stir-fry for 2–3 minutes. Add the garlic, ginger, chillies and turmeric and stir-fry for 2 minutes more.

Stir in the prawns, salt and chopped fenugreek, cover the wok and cook gently for 8–10 minutes. At the end of this cooking time lower the heat over a very low heat and leave the prawns for a few minutes before serving.

Arrange the tomato slices around the edge of a serving dish and pile the prawns in the middle, then serve immediately.

Serves 4

Preparation time: 30 minutes

Cooking time: 15 minutes

King Prawns and Eggs in Coconut Sauce

- 5 MACADAMIA NUTS, CHOPPED
- 3 FRESH RED CHILLIES, DESEEDED AND CHOPPED
- 1 SMALL ONION, CHOPPED
- 2 GARLIC CLOVES, CHOPPED
- ½ TEASPOON DRIED SHRIMP PASTE
- 2 TEASPOONS GROUND CORIANDER
- 1 TEASPOON GRATED FRESH ROOT GINGER
- 2 TABLESPOONS VEGETABLE OIL
- 625 G/1 ¼ LB UNCOOKED LARGE PRAWNS, SHELLED AND DEVEINED
- 3 RIPE TOMATOES, CHOPPED
- SALT
- 1 BAY LEAF
- 150 ML/¼ PINT THICK COCONUT MILK
- 4 HARD-BOILED EGGS, HALVED
- 75 G/3 OZ MANGETOUT, TRIMMED

Put the macadamias, chillies, onion, garlic, shrimp paste, coriander and ginger in a liquidizer or food processor and purée.

Heat the oil in a large wok and gently stir-fry the paste for about 1 minute. Add the prawns, tomatoes and salt to taste. Stir, cover and simmer for 2 minutes. Stir in the bay leaf and 150 ml/¼ pint water. Increase the heat and boil, uncovered, for 5 minutes.

Lower the heat, add the coconut milk and eggs and simmer for 5 minutes. Add the mangetout and simmer for a further 3 minutes. Transfer to a warmed serving dish and serve at once.

SERVES 4
PREPARATION TIME: 15 MINUTES
COOKING TIME: 15 MINUTES

Balti Spinach with Prawns

- 50 G/2 OZ GHEE OR BUTTER (SEE PAGE 11)
- 1 LARGE ONION, SLICED
- 2 CLOVES GARLIC, SLICED
- 1 TABLESPOON TOMATO PURÉE
- 1½ TEASPOONS GROUND CORIANDER
- 1 TEASPOON GARAM MASALA (SEE PAGE 11)
- ½ TEASPOON GROUND TURMERIC
- ½ TEASPOON CHILLI POWDER
- 1 TEASPOON GROUND GINGER
- 1 TEASPOON SALT
- 500 G/1 LB FROZEN WHOLE LEAF SPINACH
- 500 G/1 LB PEELED COOKED PRAWNS
- LEMON WEDGES, TO GARNISH

Melt the ghee or butter in a large wok or heavy-based frying pan, add the onion and garlic and fry gently for 4–5 minutes, until the onion is soft. Stir in the tomato purée and stir-fry for 1 minute. Add the spices and salt and stir-fry for a further 5 minutes.

Add the frozen spinach, breaking it up gently with a wooden spoon. Cook until the spinach has thoroughly defrosted, about 3–4 minutes, stirring frequently. Add the prawns and cook for a further 5 minutes, turning gently to coat with the spinach. Serve at once, garnished with lemon wedges.

SERVES 4

PREPARATION TIME: 10 MINUTES

COOKING TIME: 20 MINUTES

Shrimps with Spinach and Herbs

250 g/8 oz dried shrimps
3 tablespoons vegetable oil
2 onions, sliced
1 teaspoon finely chopped garlic
1 teaspoon finely chopped fresh root ginger
½ teaspoon salt
500 g/1 lb fresh spinach, trimmed and shredded
4 green chillies, chopped
2 tablespoons chopped fresh coriander
1 teaspoon chopped fresh mint
1 white radish, to garnish (optional)

Rinse the shrimps under cold running water, then soak them in cold water to cover for at least 30 minutes.

Heat the oil in a large wok and fry the onions for 5–10 minutes, until lightly browned. Add the garlic, ginger and salt, and stir-fry for a few minutes. Stir in the drained shrimps and spinach, cover the pan and cook over a medium to low heat for about 20–30 minutes, or until the shrimps are tender. Stir once or twice during cooking. The liquid from the spinach should be sufficient to tenderize the shrimps, but extra water may be added if necessary.

Stir in the chopped chillies, coriander and mint, then lower the heat to very low, cover the wok and leave for about 10 minutes.

Slice the radish into a long, spiral strip. Arrange the shrimps on a serving dish and garnish with the radish spiral, if using.

Note: Dried shrimps are obtainable from Indian and Chinese food stores and some delicatessens. Before cooking they must be soaked for at least 30 minutes otherwise they become leathery. They are usually salted, so season the dish carefully.

Serves 4
Preparation time: 30 minutes, plus 30 minutes soaking
Cooking time: 40–50 minutes

Balti Mussels

1 KG/2 LB MUSSELS
50 G/2 OZ GHEE OR BUTTER (SEE PAGE 11)
1 LARGE ONION, CHOPPED
2 GARLIC CLOVES, CHOPPED
2 TEASPOONS DESICCATED COCONUT
2 TEASPOONS SALT
1 TEASPOON GROUND TURMERIC
1 TEASPOON CHILLI POWDER
1 TEASPOON PEPPER
1 TABLESPOON VINEGAR
500 G/1 LB NATURAL YOGURT
2 TEASPOONS GARAM MASALA (SEE PAGE 11)
JUICE OF 2 LEMONS

Scrub the mussels thoroughly under cold running water and pull away the 'beard'. Soak them for 30 minutes. Discard any mussels that are not tightly shut or do not close quickly when tapped.

Heat the ghee or butter in a large wok, add the onion and garlic and fry for 5 minutes, until the onion is soft. Add the coconut with the salt and stir-fry until lightly browned. Stir in the turmeric, chilli powder and pepper and fry for 1 minute. Add the vinegar and mussels, cover and bring to the boil; cook for about 5 minutes, or until the shells open, then remove from the heat.

Remove the empty half shells and discard. Arrange the mussels in their half shells in a large serving dish. Pour the cooking liquid into a liquidizer or food processor with the yogurt and garam masala and blend for 1 minute. Reheat until hot but not boiling. Pour over the mussels, sprinkle with lemon juice and serve at once.

Serves 6
Preparation time: 40 minutes
Cooking time: 10–15 minutes

Balti Crab

50 G/2 OZ GHEE OR BUTTER (SEE PAGE 11)
1 ONION, FINELY CHOPPED
1 GARLIC CLOVE, CRUSHED
2.5 CM/1 INCH PIECE FRESH ROOT GINGER, PEELED AND GRATED
1 TABLESPOON CHOPPED FRESH CORIANDER LEAVES, PLUS EXTRA, TO GARNISH
1 TEASPOON GROUND NUTMEG
1 TEASPOON CHILLI POWDER
1 TEASPOON SUGAR
425 G/14 OZ CAN TOMATOES, CHOPPED, WITH THE JUICE
500 G/1 LB COOKED CRAB MEAT (FRESH, CANNED OR FROZEN AND DEFROSTED)
SALT

Heat the ghee or butter in a large wok or heavy-based frying pan and fry the onion for 4–5 minutes, or until just soft. Add the garlic, ginger, coriander, nutmeg, chilli, sugar and salt to taste, and stir-fry for a further 2–3 minutes. Add the tomatoes and fry gently for 25–30 minutes, until the mixture is reduced to a thick sauce.

Gently fold the crab meat into the sauce. Cover the wok and simmer very gently for 5–7 minutes. Serve at once, garnished with chopped coriander.

SERVES 4
PREPARATION TIME: 10 MINUTES
COOKING TIME: 35–40 MINUTES

Balti Crab Korma

1 FRESH COCONUT
75 G/3 OZ GHEE OR BUTTER (SEE PAGE 11)
1 LARGE ONION, THINLY SLICED
4 GARLIC CLOVES, THINLY SLICED
7 CM/3 INCH PIECE FRESH ROOT GINGER, PEELED AND THINLY SLICED
2 TEASPOONS FENUGREEK SEEDS
2 TEASPOONS PEPPER
2 TEASPOONS CHILLI POWDER
2 TEASPOONS GROUND CORIANDER
1 TEASPOON GROUND TURMERIC
1 TEASPOON SALT
500 G/1 LB NATURAL YOGURT
300 ML/½ PINT MILK
500 G/1 LB COOKED CRAB MEAT (FRESH, CANNED OR FROZEN AND DEFROSTED)
2 TABLESPOONS CHOPPED FRESH CORIANDER LEAVES, TO GARNISH

Make holes in the eyes of the coconut, drain out the liquid and reserve. Crack open the coconut and separate the meat from the shell. Thinly slice a quarter of the coconut and reserve. Put the remaining coconut in a liquidizer or food processor and process until chopped.

Transfer the chopped coconut to a bowl, pour over 600 ml/1 pint boiling water, stir for 5 minutes, then strain through a sieve lined with muslin set over a bowl. Gather up the muslin and squeeze out as much of the coconut milk as possible. Discard the coconut from inside the cloth. Stir the reserved liquid from the coconut into the coconut milk and set aside.

Melt the ghee or butter in a wok, add the onion, garlic and ginger and fry for 4 minutes, or until soft. Add the fenugreek seeds, pepper, chilli powder, coriander, turmeric and salt. Fry for 2–3 minutes, then add the coconut milk. Put the yogurt and fresh milk in a bowl and stir until mixed. Stir slowly into the wok, bring to below boiling point and simmer for 6 minutes. Stir in the crab and sliced coconut. Cook for 5 minutes, sprinkle with coriander and serve.

SERVES 6
PREPARATION TIME: 30 MINUTES
COOKING TIME: 15–20 MINUTES

Balti Seafood Curry

1–2 tablespoons vegetable oil
2 onions, finely chopped
2 garlic cloves, crushed
1 green pepper, deseeded and sliced
2 tablespoons curry powder
2 teaspoons chilli powder
25 g/1 oz plain flour
500 g/1 lb white fish fillets, skinned and cubed
125 g/4 oz cooked mussels
125 g/4 oz peeled cooked prawns
4 tomatoes, peeled, deseeded and quartered
salt and pepper

To garnish:
cooked prawns in their shells
a few sprigs of coriander

Heat the oil in a large wok or heavy-based frying pan, add the onions, garlic and pepper and fry until soft but not browned. Add the spices and flour and cook gently for about 2–3 minutes. Gradually add 600 ml/1 pint hot water, stirring all the time. Bring the mixture to the boil, lower the heat to a gentle simmer, then add the white fish and cook for 15 minutes.

Add the cooked mussels, prawns and tomatoes, season to taste with salt and pepper and simmer for a further 5–10 minutes.

Garnish with whole prawns and coriander sprigs and serve at once.

Serves 4–6
Preparation time: 20 minutes
Cooking time: 25–30 minutes

Madras Mackerel

25 g/1 oz dried tamarind, soaked in 150 ml/¼ pint boiling water for 30 minutes
2 tablespoons vegetable oil
1 onion, finely chopped
3 garlic cloves, crushed
1 teaspoon chilli powder
¼ teaspoon ground turmeric
1½ teaspoons ground coriander
½ teaspoon cumin seeds, dry-roasted and ground
½ teaspoon mustard seeds, dry-roasted and ground
½ teaspoon fenugreek seeds, dry-roasted and ground
15 g/½ oz desiccated coconut
4–5 curry leaves
250 g/8 oz can chopped tomatoes
500 g/1 lb mackerel, cleaned and cut into 5 cm/2 inch pieces
1 fresh green chilli, deseeded and very finely chopped
salt

To garnish:
1 onion, finely chopped
2 tablespoons vegetable oil
1 teaspoon cumin seeds
chopped fresh coriander leaves

Strain the tamarind liquid through a wire sieve set over a small bowl, pressing to extract as much pulp as possible.

Heat the oil in a wok and fry the onion for 5–10 minutes, until the onion is lightly browned. Add the garlic, chilli powder, turmeric, coriander, cumin, mustard seeds, fenugreek, coconut and curry leaves. Gently fry for 30 seconds. Add the tamarind pulp and the tomatoes, and simmer gently for 1 minute.

Add the mackerel, then the chilli and a pinch of salt. Cover and cook for 20–30 minutes. If necessary add a little water.

To garnish, fry the onion in the oil until browned. Add the cumin seeds and as soon as they crackle, pour over the fish curry. Sprinkle with chopped coriander and serve.

Serves 4–6
Preparation time: about 30 minutes, plus soaking
Cooking time: 40–50 minutes

Tamarind Fish

- 50 g/2 oz dried tamarind, soaked in 6 tablespoons boiling water for 30 minutes
- 4 tablespoons vegetable oil
- 750 g/1½ lb monkfish or other firm white fish, cubed
- flour for dusting
- 1 onion, chopped
- 4 fresh green chillies, deseeded and finely chopped
- 2 garlic cloves, crushed
- 1 teaspoon ground cumin
- ½–1 teaspoon chilli powder
- 1 tablespoon vinegar
- salt

Strain the tamarind liquid through a wire sieve set over a small bowl, pressing to squeeze out as much liquid as possible. Discard the tamarind pulp and reserve the liquid.

Heat the oil in a large wok or heavy-based frying pan. Lightly dust the fish with flour, add to the wok and fry quickly on all sides. Remove the fish with a slotted spoon and set aside.

Add the onion to the wok and fry until soft and golden. Add the tamarind liquid, chillies, garlic, cumin, chilli powder, and salt to taste and cook for 10 minutes. Add the vinegar and the fish and any juices. Simmer, uncovered, for about 5 minutes; be careful not to overcook. Serve at once.

Serves 4–6

Preparation time: 20 minutes, plus 30 minutes soaking

Cooking time: about 30 minutes

Fish Molee

750 G/1½ LB COD FILLET, SKINNED
2 TABLESPOONS FLOUR
4 TABLESPOONS VEGETABLE OIL
2 ONIONS, SLICED
2 GARLIC CLOVES, CRUSHED
1 TEASPOON GROUND TURMERIC
4 FRESH GREEN CHILLIES, FINELY CHOPPED
2 TABLESPOONS LEMON JUICE
175 ML/6 FL OZ THICK COCONUT MILK
SALT

Cut the fish into 4–6 pieces and dust with the flour. Heat the oil in a large wok or heavy-based frying pan, add the fish and fry quickly on both sides. Remove the fish with a slotted spoon and set aside.

Add the onions and garlic to the wok and fry gently for about 5–10 minutes, until the onion is soft and golden. Add the turmeric, chillies, lemon juice, coconut milk, and salt to taste and simmer, uncovered, for 10 minutes or until thickened.

Add the fish and any juices, spoon over the sauce and cook gently for 2–3 minutes, until tender. Serve at once.

SERVES 4–6
PREPARATION TIME: 20 MINUTES
COOKING TIME: ABOUT 30 MINUTES

Fish with Lime and Coconut Curry

750 G/1½ LB WHITE FISH FILLETS
1 LIME
¼ TEASPOON MUSTARD POWDER
½ TEASPOON CHILLI POWDER
A PINCH OF SALT
FLOUR FOR DUSTING
VEGETABLE OIL FOR SHALLOW FRYING
25 G/1 OZ GHEE OR BUTTER (SEE PAGE 11)
1 LARGE ONION, CHOPPED
1 FRESH GREEN CHILLI, FINELY CHOPPED
2.5 CM/1 INCH PIECE FRESH ROOT GINGER, FINELY CHOPPED
1 GARLIC CLOVE, CRUSHED
1 TEASPOON CURRY POWDER
250 ML/8 FL OZ COCONUT MILK

Cut the fish into 5 cm/2 inch pieces and place in a large shallow dish. Cut the zest from the lime into thin strips and reserve. Squeeze the juice from the lime and mix with the mustard, chilli powder and salt. Pour the lime juice mixture over the fish and leave to marinate for 2–3 hours.

Drain the fish pieces, dust them with flour and fry in hot oil in a wok until they are golden brown on both sides. Remove the fish with a slotted spoon and set aside.

Add the ghee or butter to the wok, then add the onion, chilli, ginger, garlic and curry powder and fry until golden brown. Stir in the coconut milk and bring to the boil, stirring. Then add the fried fish and simmer gently, uncovered, for 5 minutes. Serve immediately, sprinkled with the reserved lime zest.

SERVES 4–6

PREPARATION TIME: 20 MINUTES, PLUS 2–3 HOURS MARINATING

COOKING TIME: 20 MINUTES

Balti Fish

40 G/1½ OZ GHEE (SEE PAGE 11) OR
3 TABLESPOONS VEGETABLE OIL
2 ONIONS, CHOPPED
25 G/1 OZ FRESH ROOT GINGER, PEELED AND CRUSHED
4–5 GARLIC CLOVES, CRUSHED
½ TEASPOON GROUND TURMERIC
1 TEASPOON CHILLI POWDER
1 TEASPOON GROUND CUMIN
1 TEASPOON GROUND CORIANDER
1 TEASPOON GARAM MASALA (SEE PAGE 11)
750 G/1½ LB WHITE FISH FILLETS, CUT INTO 2.5 CM/1 INCH PIECES
250 G/8 OZ CAN CHOPPED TOMATOES
1 TEASPOON SALT
1 FRESH GREEN CHILLI, HALVED AND DESEEDED

TO GARNISH:
1 GREEN PEPPER, DESEEDED AND FINELY CHOPPED
CHOPPED FRESH CORIANDER LEAVES

Heat the ghee or oil in a large wok or heavy-based frying pan and fry the onions for 5–10 minutes, until lightly browned. Add the ginger, garlic, turmeric, chilli powder, cumin, ground coriander and garam masala. Stir-fry for 15 seconds, then add the fish pieces and stir gently.

Add the tomatoes, salt and chilli. Cover and simmer gently for 5–10 minutes, or until the fish is tender. Remove from the heat and add the chopped green pepper and coriander. Remove the chilli if preferred, and serve at once.

SERVES 4–6
PREPARATION TIME: 15 MINUTES
COOKING TIME: ABOUT 20 MINUTES

Balti Fish with Coconut

3 TABLESPOONS DESICCATED COCONUT
4 COD STEAKS, ABOUT 3 CM/1¼ INCHES THICK
3 TABLESPOONS VEGETABLE OIL
1 TEASPOON MUSTARD SEEDS
2 ONIONS, ROUGHLY CHOPPED
1 GREEN PEPPER, DESEEDED AND CHOPPED
2 LARGE GARLIC CLOVES, CRUSHED
2.5 CM/1 INCH PIECE FRESH ROOT GINGER, GRATED
½ TEASPOON CHILLI POWDER
1 TABLESPOON CORNFLOUR
½ TEASPOON SALT
½–1 TEASPOON GARAM MASALA (SEE PAGE 11)
1 TABLESPOON DESICCATED COCONUT, LIGHTLY TOASTED
2 TABLESPOONS LEMON JUICE
FRESH CORIANDER, TO GARNISH

Put the coconut in a sieve set over a bowl, pour over 300 ml/½ pint boiling water and leave to infuse for 20 minutes, pressing the coconut with the back of a wooden spoon to extract as much liquid as possible.

Pat the cod steaks dry with kitchen paper. Heat the oil in a wok. Add the mustard seeds, and as soon as they pop, add the onions and green pepper and fry for 3–4 minutes, until beginning to soften. Add the garlic, ginger and chilli powder and stir-fry for 2 minutes. Add the cornflour and stir until it is thoroughly combined.

Stir in the coconut liquid, salt and garam masala. Bring the mixture slowly to the boil over a low heat.

Add the cod to the wok. Spoon over the sauce, cover and simmer gently for 25 minutes, or until the fish is firm and flakes easily.

Sprinkle the toasted coconut and lemon juice over the fish, and serve at once, garnished with sprigs of coriander.

SERVES 4
PREPARATION TIME: 25 MINUTES
COOKING TIME: 30 MINUTES

Fish in Creamy Balti Sauce

4 PLAICE FILLETS
150 ML/¼ PINT DOUBLE CREAM
GRATED RIND AND JUICE OF 1 LEMON
SALT
A FEW SPRIGS OF FRESH CORIANDER LEAVES, TO GARNISH
BALTI SAUCE:
75 G/3 OZ GHEE OR BUTTER (SEE PAGE 11)
1 LARGE ONION, FINELY CHOPPED
2 GARLIC CLOVES, CRUSHED
50 G/2 OZ PIECE OF FRESH GINGER, PEELED AND CHOPPED
1 TABLESPOON GROUND CORIANDER
1 TEASPOON GARAM MASALA (SEE PAGE 11)
1 TEASPOON CHILLI POWDER
1 TEASPOON GROUND CARDAMOM
425 G/14 OZ CAN TOMATOES, CHOPPED WITH THE JUICE
4 TABLESPOONS TOMATO PURÉE
2 TEASPOONS SUGAR

Wash the fish fillets and pat dry with kitchen paper. Place the fish, slightly overlapping, in a large shallow ovenproof dish.

Make the Balti sauce; heat the butter in a wok and fry the onion until golden. Add the garlic and ginger and fry for a few seconds. Add the spices and stir-fry for 2 minutes. Stir in the tomatoes and tomato purée and fry for 2 minutes more.

Add the sugar, 150 ml/¼ pint water and salt; stir well. Partly cover, and cook for 15 minutes, or until the sauce is thick and most of the liquid has evaporated.

Mix the Balti sauce, cream, lemon rind and juice together and pour over the fish. Cover and cook in a preheated oven, 180°C (350°F), Gas Mark 4, for 25–30 minutes. Serve garnished with coriander.

SERVES 4
PREPARATION TIME: 25 MINUTES
COOKING TIME: 1 HOUR

POULTRY

BALTIS

CHICKEN IS A VERSATILE AND POPULAR MAIN COURSE IN INDIAN RESTAURANTS, AND BALTIHOUSES ARE NO EXCEPTION. MILD, CREAMY KORMAS, FRUITY AND NUTTY CURRIES, AND SPICY HOT DISHES CAN ALL BE COOKED IN A BALTI PAN. DUCK IS BEST RESERVED FOR A TANGY VINDALOO, OR DISHES WITH TOMATOES OR PINEAPPLE, BUT OTHER POULTRY CAN BE SUBSTITUTED FOR CHICKEN: TRY PHEASANT, QUAIL OR TURKEY.

Balti Chicken Vindaloo

1½ teaspoons ground coriander
1½ teaspoons ground cumin
¼ teaspoon black onion seeds (kalonji)
¼ teaspoon fenugreek seeds
¼ teaspoon mustard seeds
2.5 cm/1 inch piece cinnamon stick
3 cloves
¾ teaspoon black pepper
2 tablespoons desiccated coconut
2 tablespoons unsalted peanuts
6 tablespoons vinegar
2 garlic cloves, crushed
1 teaspoon chopped fresh root ginger
½ teaspoon ground turmeric
1½ teaspoons chilli powder
2 teaspoons salt
1.5 kg/3 lb chicken, skinned and cut into pieces
3 tablespoons vegetable oil
12 curry leaves
1 teaspoon cumin seeds
chopped fresh coriander leaves, to garnish

Roast and grind the first 10 ingredients. Mix in the vinegar, garlic, ginger, turmeric, chilli powder and salt, and spread the mixture over the chicken pieces. Leave to marinate overnight.

Heat the oil in a large wok, then add the curry leaves and cumin seeds. Cook for about 10 seconds, then add the chicken and cook, turning once or twice, for 15 minutes. Cover and continue cooking for a further 15–20 minutes or until the chicken is tender, adding a little water from time to time to keep the chicken moist. Leave over a very low heat for a few minutes before serving, garnished with the chopped coriander.

Serves 4–6

Preparation time: 20 minutes, plus overnight marinating

Cooking time: 30–40 minutes

Balti Chicken

6 tablespoons vegetable oil
1 onion, chopped
½ teaspoon ground turmeric
1 teaspoon ground coriander
1 teaspoon ground cumin
1 teaspoon chilli powder
750 g/1½ lb skinned and boned chicken, cubed
1 kg/2 lb tomatoes, chopped
1 large green pepper, deseeded and cut into squares
4–6 garlic cloves, chopped
2 fresh green chillies, chopped
salt
To garnish:
2 tomatoes, quartered
fresh coriander sprigs

Heat the oil in a large wok or heavy-based saucepan, add the onion and fry until soft. Mix the turmeric, coriander, cumin and chilli powder with 2 tablespoons of water. Stir this spice mixture into the onions and cook until the liquid has dried up, about 3–4 minutes. Add the chicken and fry on all sides, then add the tomatoes and a pinch of salt to taste. Cover and cook for 15 minutes.

Add the green pepper, garlic and chillies. Cook, uncovered, until all the tomato juices have evaporated and the chicken is cooked through. Serve hot, garnished with the tomatoes and coriander sprigs.

Serves 4–6
Preparation time: 20 minutes
Cooking time: 30 minutes

Special Spiced Balti Chicken

- ½ teaspoon black peppercorns
- ½ teaspoon black onion seeds (kalonji)
- ½ teaspoon fennel seeds
- 2 tablespoons vegetable oil
- 1 onion, chopped
- 2.5 cm/1 inch piece fresh root ginger, crushed
- 1 garlic clove, crushed
- 1 tablespoon garam masala (see page 11)
- 1 teaspoon ground coriander
- 1 teaspoon ground cumin
- 1 teaspoon chilli powder
- 1 teaspoon ground turmeric
- 50 g/2 oz coconut milk powder
- 1 tablespoon lemon juice
- 6 cardamom pods, bruised
- 5 cm/2 inch piece cinnamon stick
- 1 bay leaf
- 1 kg/2 lb skinned and boned chicken thighs, cut into bite-sized pieces
- 4 ripe tomatoes, skinned, deseeded and chopped roughly
- ¼ teaspoon sugar
- salt
- fresh coriander leaves, to garnish

Dry-fry the peppercorns, black onion and fennel seeds over a gentle heat, stirring for 3 minutes until fragrant, then grind to a powder.

Heat the oil, add the onion, ginger and garlic and fry, stirring for 5 minutes until soft. Add the roasted spices, garam masala, coriander, cumin, chilli powder and turmeric. Stir-fry for 3 minutes, then add 450 ml/¾ pint water, the coconut milk powder, lemon juice and ½ teaspoon salt. Bring to the boil, stirring, then add the cardamoms, cinnamon and bay leaf. Simmer, stirring occasionally, for 15–20 minutes, until a glaze forms on top of the liquid.

Add the chicken, tomatoes and sugar and stir. Cover and cook for 20 minutes, or until the chicken is cooked. Remove and discard the bay leaf and cinnamon and serve hot, garnished with coriander.

Serves 4–6

Preparation time: 30 minutes

Cooking time: 30 minutes

Balti Pineapple Chicken

2 ONIONS, QUARTERED

2 GARLIC CLOVES

3.5 CM/1½ INCH PIECE FRESH ROOT GINGER, PEELED AND CHOPPED

1 TEASPOON GROUND TURMERIC

1 TABLESPOON GROUND CORIANDER

1–2 TEASPOONS CHILLI POWDER

2 TABLESPOONS PAPRIKA

1 TEASPOON SUGAR

1 TEASPOON SALT

2 TABLESPOONS VEGETABLE OIL

8 CHICKEN THIGHS, SKINNED

125 G/4 OZ CASHEW NUTS, SOAKED IN BOILING WATER FOR 1 HOUR

6 CURRY LEAVES

4 FRESH GREEN CHILLIES, SLIT AND DESEEDED

1 PINEAPPLE, CUBED

JUICE OF ½–1 LEMON

Purée the onions, garlic, ginger, turmeric, coriander, chilli powder, paprika, sugar and salt in a liquidizer or food processor.

Heat the oil in a wok or heavy-based frying pan, add the spice paste and fry for 10 minutes. Add the chicken pieces and stir-fry for 5 minutes. Pour in 300 ml/½ pint water and bring to simmering point. Add the drained nuts, curry leaves and chillies, cover and simmer for 25 minutes. Add the pineapple and lemon juice to taste and simmer for a further 10 minutes. Serve hot.

SERVES 4

PREPARATION TIME: 30 MINUTES, PLUS 1 HOUR SOAKING

COOKING TIME: 45 MINUTES

Chilli Chicken

- 750 g/1½ lb skinned and boned chicken breasts, cubed
- 1 teaspoon sugar
- 3–6 fresh red chillies
- 4 almonds
- 1 stem lemon grass, sliced
- 1 teaspoon ground fenugreek
- 2.5 cm/1 inch piece fresh root ginger, peeled and chopped
- 6 small red onions or shallots, sliced
- 4 garlic cloves, crushed
- 4 tablespoons vegetable oil
- salt
- shredded spring onions, to garnish

Sprinkle the chicken with the sugar. Purée the chillies with the almonds, lemon grass, fenugreek and half the ginger. Purée the remaining ginger with the onions and garlic.

Heat the oil in a wok or heavy-based frying pan and stir-fry the chilli mixture for about 1–2 minutes. Add the onion mixture and stir-fry for 1–2 minutes more. Add the chicken pieces and stir well to coat the chicken thoroughly. Add 150 ml/¼ pint water and a pinch of salt. Cover and cook gently for about 10–15 minutes, or until the chicken is cooked through.

Transfer the chicken to a serving dish and serve sprinkled with the shredded spring onions.

Serves 4–6

Preparation time: 15 minutes

Cooking time: about 15–20 minutes

Chicken Molee

3 TABLESPOONS VEGETABLE OIL
4 CHICKEN BREASTS, SKINNED, BONED AND DICED
6 CARDAMOM PODS
6 CLOVES
5 CM/2 INCH PIECE CINNAMON STICK
1 LARGE ONION, SLICED
2 GARLIC CLOVES
4 CM/1½ INCH PIECE FRESH ROOT GINGER, PEELED AND CHOPPED
3 FRESH GREEN CHILLIES, DESEEDED
JUICE OF 1 LEMON
1 TEASPOON GROUND TURMERIC
50 G/2 OZ CREAMED COCONUT
SALT

Heat the oil in a wok or heavy-based frying pan, add the chicken and stir-fry until browned on all sides. Remove with a slotted spoon and set aside.

Add the cardamoms, cloves and cinnamon stick and stir-fry for about 1 minute. Add the onion and fry until soft. Purée the garlic, ginger, chillies and lemon juice in a liquidizer or food processor. Add to the wok with the turmeric and cook for about 5 minutes.

Melt the coconut in 150 ml/¼ pint hot water and add to the wok with salt to taste. Simmer for 2 minutes, then add the reserved chicken pieces and any juices. Simmer for 15–20 minutes, or until the chicken is tender. Serve hot.

SERVES 4–6
PREPARATION TIME: 15 MINUTES
COOKING TIME: ABOUT 30 MINUTES

Chicken Masala

- 2 garlic cloves, chopped
- 5 cm/2 inch piece fresh root ginger, peeled and chopped
- 1 teaspoon ground turmeric
- 2 teaspoons cumin seeds, ground
- 1 teaspoon chilli powder
- 1 teaspoon pepper
- 3 tablespoons finely chopped fresh coriander leaves
- 500 g/1 lb natural yogurt
- 1 kg/2 lb chicken pieces, skinned
- 4 tablespoons vegetable oil
- 2 onions, chopped
- salt

Put the garlic, ginger, turmeric, cumin, chilli powder, pepper, fresh coriander, yogurt and salt to taste into a large bowl. Mix well, add the chicken pieces and leave for 4 hours, turning the chicken occasionally in the marinade.

Heat the oil in a wok or heavy-based frying pan, add the onions and fry until they are golden brown. Add the chicken and the marinade. Bring to simmering point, cover and cook for about 20 minutes, or until the chicken is cooked through. Serve hot.

Serves 4–6

Preparation time: 15 minutes, plus 4 hours marinating

Cooking time: about 35 minutes

Balti Chicken and Potatoes

2 TABLESPOONS VEGETABLE OIL
2 GARLIC CLOVES, FINELY CHOPPED
1 TEASPOON GROUND TURMERIC
1 KG/2 LB CHICKEN PIECES, SKINNED
250 G/8 OZ POTATOES, CUT INTO CUBES
250 G/8 OZ SMALL SHALLOTS, PEELED BUT LEFT WHOLE
SALT AND PEPPER

Heat the oil in a wok or heavy-based frying pan. Add the garlic and turmeric and stir-fry for about 1 minute, taking care not to let the garlic brown. Add the chicken pieces and fry for about 10 minutes, or until the chicken is well browned.

Add the potatoes and shallots and stir-fry for 2 minutes. Season with salt and pepper and add just enough water to cover the bottom of the wok. Cover and simmer gently for about 25 minutes or until tender, adding more water if necessary to prevent burning.

Uncover the wok and leave on the heat for a few minutes, or until all the liquid has evaporated. Serve hot.

SERVES 4–6
PREPARATION TIME: 10 MINUTES
COOKING TIME: 35–40 MINUTES

Chicken Dopiaza

2 TABLESPOONS VEGETABLE OIL
3 ONIONS, THINLY SLICED
¼ TEASPOON GARLIC POWDER
2 TEASPOONS GROUND CORIANDER
1 TABLESPOON GROUND CUMIN
½ TEASPOON GROUND TURMERIC
1 TEASPOON GROUND GINGER
½–1 TEASPOON CHILLI POWDER
750 G/1½ LB SKINNED AND BONED CHICKEN, CUBED
500 G/1 LB TOMATOES, SKINNED AND HALVED
375 G/12 OZ SMALL NEW POTATOES, SCRAPED
SALT AND PEPPER
CHOPPED FRESH CORIANDER, TO GARNISH

Heat the oil in a wok or heavy-based frying pan and fry the onions until they are golden brown. Mix the garlic with the spices and a little pepper. Add the spice mixture to the wok and stir-fry for about 1 minute.

Add the chicken and fry until browned on all sides, then add the tomatoes and potatoes and fry for a further 2–3 minutes.

Pour in just enough water to cover the chicken and add a pinch of salt. Bring to the boil, cover and simmer for 15 minutes, or until the potatoes are nearly tender.

Increase the heat and cook, uncovered, until the potatoes are tender and the chicken is cooked. Serve hot, garnished with coriander.

Serves 4–6
Preparation time: 20 minutes
Cooking time: 30 minutes

Chicken with Cashew Nuts

4 CHICKEN QUARTERS, SKINNED
300 ML/½ PINT CHICKEN STOCK
2 TABLESPOONS VEGETABLE OIL
2 LARGE ONIONS, FINELY CHOPPED
1 TEASPOON CHILLI POWDER
2 GARLIC CLOVES, CRUSHED
2.5 CM/1 INCH PIECE FRESH ROOT GINGER, PEELED AND FINELY CHOPPED
1 TABLESPOON CURRY POWDER
300 ML/½ PINT NATURAL YOGURT
125 G/4 OZ CASHEW NUTS, CHOPPED
SALT

Put the chicken quarters into a saucepan with the stock and simmer for about 45 minutes, or until the chicken is tender. Remove the chicken with a slotted spoon and set aside. Reserve 150 ml/¼ pint of the stock.

Heat the oil in a large wok or heavy-based frying pan and fry the onions, chilli powder, garlic, ginger and curry powder until golden. Beat the yogurt with the reserved stock. Add the yogurt mixture to the wok and bring slowly to the boil. Add the chicken and simmer for a few minutes, stirring all the time. Stir in the chopped cashew nuts and salt to taste. Serve hot.

SERVES 4
PREPARATION TIME: 15 MINUTES
COOKING TIME: 1 HOUR

Chicken Korma

- 2 tablespoons vegetable oil
- 2 fresh red chillies
- 2 onions, sliced
- 1 tablespoon ground cumin
- 1 teaspoon ground coriander
- ½ teaspoon ground turmeric
- ½ teaspoon ground ginger
- ½ teaspoon fenugreek seeds
- 1 tablespoon desiccated coconut
- 750 g/1½ lb skinned and boned chicken, cubed
- 2 cardamom pods, bruised
- 300 ml/½ pint natural yogurt
- salt
- lemon wedges to garnish

Heat the oil in a wok or heavy-based frying pan, add the whole chillies and sliced onions and fry until golden brown. Add all the spices, except the cardamoms. Stir in the coconut and stir-fry until the spices darken. Then add the chicken, cardamoms, half the yogurt and a pinch of salt. Simmer for about 20 minutes or until the chicken is cooked, adding a little water if necessary to prevent the mixture from becoming too dry.

When the chicken is cooked through, stir in the remaining yogurt and serve immediately garnished with lemon wedges.

Serves 4–6

Preparation time: 20 minutes

Cooking time: 30 minutes

Mogul-Style Chicken

3 GARLIC CLOVES, CRUSHED
½ TEASPOON GROUND GINGER
1 TEASPOON GROUND TURMERIC
1.5 KG/3 LB CHICKEN, CUT INTO 8 PIECES AND SKINNED
½ TEASPOON SAFFRON THREADS
4 TABLESPOONS HOT MILK
50 G/2 OZ GHEE OR BUTTER (SEE PAGE 11)
3 ONIONS, SLICED
2 TEASPOONS GARAM MASALA (SEE PAGE 11)
A PINCH OF GROUND MACE
150 ML/¼ PINT CHICKEN STOCK
25 G/1 OZ GROUND ALMONDS
150 ML/¼ PINT SINGLE CREAM
SALT AND PEPPER

Mix the garlic, ginger and turmeric together and rub this mixture over the chicken pieces. Add the saffron threads to the hot milk and leave to soak for 10 minutes.

Meanwhile, heat the ghee or butter in a large wok. Add the onions and sauté until they are soft and golden brown. Remove the onions with a slotted spoon and set aside.

Add the chicken pieces to the wok and fry, turning occasionally, until evenly browned. Sprinkle in the garam masala, mace and salt and pepper. Stir in the stock, onions and saffron, together with the milk. Cover and simmer gently for about 45 minutes, or until the chicken is tender.

Using a slotted spoon, transfer the chicken to a warm serving plate. Add the almonds and cream to the cooking liquid. Heat through gently, stirring constantly. Pour the sauce over the chicken and serve hot.

SERVES 4–6
PREPARATION TIME: 15 MINUTES
COOKING TIME: 1 HOUR

Chicken and Lentil Curry

250 G/8 OZ RED LENTILS (MASOOR DAL)
3 TABLESPOONS VEGETABLE OIL
2 ONIONS, FINELY CHOPPED
2 GARLIC CLOVES, CRUSHED
2.5 CM/1 INCH PIECE FRESH ROOT GINGER, PEELED AND FINELY CHOPPED
1 TABLESPOON GROUND CORIANDER
1 TEASPOON GROUND CUMIN
½ TEASPOON GROUND TURMERIC
½ TEASPOON GROUND CLOVES
2 TEASPOONS CHILLI POWDER
750 G/1½ LB CHICKEN THIGHS, SKINNED
SALT
LEMON WEDGES, TO GARNISH

Wash the lentils thoroughly and soak in 600 ml/1 pint cold water for 1 hour. Drain well and then boil for about 1 hour, until soft. Rinse the lentils thoroughly in fresh water, drain and set aside.

Heat the oil in a wok or heavy-based frying pan, add the onions, garlic and ginger and fry for about 5 minutes. Add the spices and salt to taste and fry gently for 10 minutes; if the mixture becomes too dry, add 2 tablespoons of water. Add the chicken thighs and fry until they are golden all over. Add the cooked lentils, cover and simmer for about 30 minutes, or until the chicken is tender. Serve hot, garnished with lemon wedges.

SERVES 4–6
PREPARATION TIME: 15 MINUTES, PLUS 1 HOUR SOAKING
COOKING TIME: ABOUT 2 HOURS

Kashmiri Chicken

50 G/2 OZ GHEE OR BUTTER (SEE PAGE 11)
3 LARGE ONIONS, FINELY SLICED
10 PEPPERCORNS
10 CARDAMOM PODS
5 CM/2 INCH PIECE CINNAMON STICK
5 CM/2 INCH PIECE FRESH ROOT GINGER, PEELED AND CHOPPED
2 GARLIC CLOVES, FINELY CHOPPED
1 TEASPOON CHILLI POWDER
2 TEASPOONS PAPRIKA
1.5 KG/3 LB CHICKEN PIECES, SKINNED
250 ML/8 FL OZ NATURAL YOGURT
TO GARNISH:
LIME WEDGES
SPRIGS OF PARSLEY

Melt the ghee or butter in a wok. Add the onions, peppercorns, cardamoms and cinnamon and fry until the onions are golden. Add the ginger, garlic, chilli powder, paprika and salt to taste and fry for 2 minutes, stirring occasionally.

Add the chicken pieces and fry until they are evenly browned. Gradually add the yogurt, stirring constantly. Cover and cook for about 30 minutes, or until the chicken is cooked. Serve hot, garnished with lime wedges and sprigs of parsley.

SERVES 4–6
PREPARATION TIME: 10 MINUTES
COOKING TIME: ABOUT 40 MINUTES

Balti Chicken and Tomatoes

2 tablespoons vegetable oil
½ teaspoon cumin seeds
½ teaspoon ground cinnamon
seeds from 2 cardamom pods, crushed
2 onions, chopped
1 heaped teaspoon chopped fresh root ginger
½ teaspoon pepper
2 garlic cloves, crushed
3–4 chicken breasts, skinned and cut into slivers
1 tablespoon soy sauce
425 g/14 oz can chopped tomatoes
1–2 teaspoons sugar
½ teaspoon garam masala (see page 11)

Heat the oil in a wok or heavy-based frying pan and fry the cumin seeds, cinnamon and cardamom seeds for 1 minute. Add the onions, ginger, pepper and garlic and fry for 2 minutes.

Add the chicken and stir-fry for about 5 minutes, or until they are evenly browned. Add soy sauce, the tomatoes with their juice, and sugar to taste. Bring to the boil, lower the heat and stir in the garam masala. Serve at once.

Serves 4
Preparation time: 10 minutes
Cooking time: 10 minutes

Balti Shredded Chicken

- 2 fresh green chillies, deseeded and chopped
- 3 garlic cloves
- 50 g/2 oz fresh root ginger, peeled
- 1 large onion, roughly chopped
- 1 tablespoon vinegar
- 4 chicken breasts, skinned and cut into slivers
- 3 teaspoons ground cumin
- 2 teaspoons pepper
- 40 g/1½ oz ghee or butter (see page 11)
- 2 green peppers, deseeded and sliced
- juice of 1 lemon
- salt

Grind the green chillies, garlic, ginger, onion and vinegar to a paste. Place the shredded chicken and the paste in a large bowl, mix well, coating the chicken thoroughly, then cover and set aside in the refrigerator for 1 hour to marinate.

Add the cumin, pepper and a pinch of salt to the marinated mixture and mix well. Heat the ghee or butter in a large wok or heavy-based frying pan, add the chicken mixture and stir-fry over a gentle heat for 10–15 minutes.

Uncover the wok and add the sliced green pepper. Stir-fry for a further 10 minutes or until the mixture is fairly dry and the chicken is cooked. Sprinkle with lemon juice before serving.

Serves 4–6

Preparation time: 20 minutes, plus 1 hour marinating

Cooking time: 25–30 minutes

Tomato Chicken Curry

- 3 tablespoons vegetable oil
- 1 onion, sliced
- 2.5 cm / 1 inch piece cinnamon stick
- 4 small green cardamom pods
- 2 fresh green chillies, halved and deseeded
- 50 g/2 oz fresh root ginger, peeled and finely sliced
- 6–7 garlic cloves, sliced
- 1½ kg/3 lb chicken, cut into 8 pieces and skinned
- 2 teaspoons ground cumin
- 3–4 sprigs fresh coriander leaves, chopped
- 425 g/14 oz can chopped tomatoes
- salt

Heat the oil in a large wok or heavy-based frying pan and fry the onion until lightly browned. Add the cinnamon, cardamoms and chillies and fry for 1 minute, then add the sliced ginger and garlic. Fry for 30 seconds, add the chicken pieces and fry for a further 10–15 minutes, turning frequently.

Add the cumin and coriander leaves and fry for 1–2 minutes, then stir in the chopped tomatoes and salt to taste. Cover and cook over a gentle heat for 30–35 minutes, until the chicken is tender. Serve hot.

Serves 8

Preparation time: 30 minutes

Cooking time: 1 hour–1 hour 10 minutes

Tandoori Chicken

8 CHICKEN QUARTERS, SKINNED
JUICE OF 2 LEMONS
2 TEASPOONS SALT
MARINADE:
10 CLOVES
2 TEASPOONS CORIANDER SEEDS
2 TEASPOONS CUMIN SEEDS
SEEDS OF 10 CARDAMOM PODS
2 ONIONS, CHOPPED
4 GARLIC CLOVES, CHOPPED
7 CM/3 INCH PIECE FRESH ROOT GINGER, PEELED AND CHOPPED
2 TEASPOONS CHILLI POWDER
2 TEASPOONS PEPPER
1½ TEASPOONS GROUND TURMERIC
350 ML/12 FL OZ NATURAL YOGURT
ORANGE OR RED FOOD COLOURING (OPTIONAL)

Wash the chicken and pat dry with kitchen paper. Make deep slashes in each piece, then place in a bowl and sprinkle with lemon juice and salt. Rub this mixture over the chicken, cover and leave in a cool place for 1 hour.

Meanwhile, prepare the marinade: spread the cloves, coriander, cumin and cardamom seeds on a baking sheet and roast in a preheated oven, 200°C (400°F), Gas Mark 6, for 10 minutes. Remove from the oven and cool, then grind coarsely in a mortar. Place the onions, garlic and ginger in a liquidizer or food processor and sprinkle with the chilli powder, pepper and turmeric. Add the yogurt and ground roasted spices, strain in the lemon juice from the chicken and blend until smooth. Add a little food colouring, if liked.

Arrange the chicken pieces in a single layer in a roasting tin and pour over the marinade. Cover and leave the chicken to marinate in the refrigerator for 24 hours, turning the pieces over occasionally.

Place the roasting tin in a preheated oven, 200°C (400°F), Gas Mark 6, and roast for 20 minutes. Transfer to a barbecue or preheated grill and cook until the outside is crisp. Serve hot or cold.

SERVES 8
PREPARATION TIME: ABOUT 40 MINUTES, PLUS 24 HOURS MARINATING
COOKING TIME: ABOUT 25 MINUTES

Tandoori Chicken Masala

1 KG/2 LB CHICKEN, CUT INTO PIECES AND SKINNED
JUICE OF 1 LEMON
1 GARLIC CLOVE, CRUSHED
½ TEASPOON GROUND CORIANDER
½ TEASPOON CHILLI POWDER
½ TEASPOON GROUND FENUGREEK
1 TEASPOON PAPRIKA
2.5 CM/1 INCH PIECE OF FRESH ROOT GINGER, FINELY CHOPPED
½ TEASPOON SALT
1 TEASPOON PEPPER
2 TABLESPOONS VEGETABLE OIL

SAUCE:
50 G/2 OZ GHEE OR BUTTER (SEE PAGE 11)
1 TEASPOON SALT
½ TEASPOON SUGAR
500 G/1 LB TOMATOES, SKINNED AND QUARTERED
1 TABLESPOON GARAM MASALA (SEE PAGE 11)
3 TABLESPOONS DOUBLE CREAM

Wash the chicken and pat dry with kitchen paper. Make deep cuts in each piece and place in a bowl. Mix the next 9 ingredients and rub the mixture over the chicken pieces. Leave in a cool place for 4–5 hours, or overnight, to marinate.

Place the chicken pieces and the marinade in a roasting tin and baste with the oil. Place in a preheated oven, 200°C (400°F), Gas Mark 6, for about 30 minutes. Baste with the juices several times during cooking.

To make the sauce, melt the ghee or butter in a wok and add the salt, sugar and tomatoes. Cook, uncovered, for about 15 minutes, stirring occasionally. Purée the mixture briefly in a liquidizer or food processor, or pass through a sieve. Return the sauce to the wok and add the garam masala. Simmer for 10 minutes, then remove from the heat and stir in the cream.

Add the cooked chicken pieces to the sauce and heat through but do not boil. Serve hot.

SERVES 4–6
PREPARATION TIME: ABOUT 30 MINUTES, PLUS 4–5 HOURS MARINATING
COOKING TIME: ABOUT 30 MINUTES

Baked Red Pepper Chicken

4 tablespoons vegetable oil
4 garlic cloves, chopped
1 tablespoon cumin seeds
1 kg/2 lb tomatoes, chopped
1 teaspoon salt
4 chicken quarters, skinned
1 beetroot, cooked and chopped
1 red pepper, deseeded and chopped
A few small fresh red chillies, to garnish (optional)

Heat the oil in a wok or heavy-based frying pan, add the garlic and fry for 1–2 minutes, then add the cumin seeds, tomatoes and salt. Cook until the tomato pulp is reduced by half.

Meanwhile, place the chicken pieces on a large piece of foil in a roasting tin. Add the chopped beetroot and red pepper to the tomato mixture and spoon it evenly over the chicken. Wrap the foil around the chicken and cook in a preheated oven, 190°C (375°F), Gas Mark 5, for 40–60 minutes. When the chicken is cooked all the juices should have evaporated. Serve hot, garnished with red chillies, if you like.

Serves 4
Preparation time: 10 minutes
Cooking time: about 1¼ hours

Sour Lime Chicken

2 DRIED LIMES
6 TABLESPOONS VEGETABLE OIL
12 CURRY LEAVES
1.5 KG/3 LB CHICKEN, CUT INTO SMALL PIECES AND SKINNED
2 ONIONS, SLICED
2 GARLIC CLOVES, CHOPPED
½ TEASPOON CHOPPED FRESH ROOT GINGER
¼ TEASPOON GROUND TURMERIC
1 TEASPOON CHILLI POWDER
3 TABLESPOONS TOMATO PURÉE
1½ TEASPOONS SALT
1 TABLESPOON CHOPPED GREEN PEPPER

Using a sharp knife, make 2 holes in the dried limes, then soak them in 450 ml/¾ pint water for at least 2 hours. Place another bowl or saucer on top to prevent the fruit from floating.

Heat the oil in a wok with 4 curry leaves. Add the chicken pieces, 2–3 at a time, and fry quickly, turning frequently, to seal them on all sides. Remove from the wok and set aside.

In the same oil, fry the onions until they are soft. Add the garlic, ginger, turmeric and chilli powder and stir-fry for 2–3 minutes. Add the tomato purée, the remaining curry leaves, the soaked limes (with their soaking water) and salt. Return the chicken to the wok and bring slowly to the boil. Cover and simmer over a low heat for about 45 minutes, or until the chicken is cooked through.

Add the green pepper and leave the wok, covered, over a very low heat for a few minutes. Serve hot.

Note: Dried limes can be obtained from Indian shops. They are easy to make – just leave fresh limes on the windowsill until brown and hard (about 2 months). They require lengthy soaking before cooking, but they give the dish a distinctive flavour.

The dried limes can be stored for several months in an airtight container in a cool, dry place.

SERVES 4–6

PREPARATION TIME: ABOUT 20 MINUTES, PLUS 2 HOURS SOAKING

COOKING TIME: ABOUT 1 HOUR

Chicken Smothered in Ginger

4 TABLESPOONS VEGETABLE OIL
5 CM/2 INCH PIECE FRESH ROOT GINGER, PEELED AND FINELY SLICED
4 FRESH GREEN CHILLIES, CUT LENGTHWAYS INTO THIN SLIVERS
1.5 KG/3 LB CHICKEN, CUT INTO SMALL PIECES AND SKINNED
3 ONIONS, CHOPPED
1½ TEASPOONS SALT

TO GARNISH:
1 LIME, SLICED
1–2 FRESH GREEN CHILLIES, FINELY SLICED

Heat the oil in a large wok and add 4–5 slices of ginger and a sprinkling of fresh chilli. Add the chicken pieces 2–3 at a time, and cook quickly, turning them over once or twice to seal the meat on all sides without browning it. Remove the chicken and set aside.

Add the onions to the wok and fry gently until soft but not browned. Add a little more ginger and chillies, and the salt, and replace the chicken. Pour in 300 ml/½ pint water. Bring to the boil, then cover and simmer for 15–20 minutes, or until tender.

Increase the heat, uncover the wok and continue to cook, stirring frequently, adding further sprinklings of chilli and ginger from time to time. When most of the liquid has evaporated and the chicken is well glazed, add any remaining ginger and chillies. Serve at once, garnished with lime slices and fresh chillies.

SERVES 4–6
PREPARATION TIME: 20 MINUTES
COOKING TIME: ABOUT 35 MINUTES

Chicken Cider Curry

2 tablespoons vegetable oil
15 g/½ oz ghee or butter (see page 11)
4 chicken quarters, skinned
1 onion, sliced
1 apple, cored and sliced
1½ tablespoons curry powder
1 tablespoon plain flour
150 ml/¼ pint stock
150 ml/¼ pint dry cider
2 tablespoons sultanas
2 tablespoons single cream
few drops of lemon juice
salt and pepper
a few parsley sprigs, to garnish

Heat the oil and ghee in a large wok or heavy-based frying pan. Fry the chicken quarters until they are golden brown on all sides, then remove and keep warm.

Add the onion to the wok and fry gently until soft. Add the apple and continue cooking for 2–3 minutes, then stir in the curry powder and flour and cook for a further 2 minutes. Blend in the stock and cider, season with salt and pepper and bring to the boil, stirring constantly. Add the sultanas, cover the wok and simmer for about 30 minutes.

Using a slotted spoon, transfer the chicken to a warm serving dish. Add the cream and lemon juice to the sauce, stir well, then pour over the chicken and serve, garnished with parsley.

Serves 4
Preparation time: 15 minutes
Cooking time: 45 minutes

Chicken Tikka Masala

4 chicken breasts, skinned, boned and cubed
juice of 1 lemon
1½ teaspoons salt
2 teaspoons pepper
1 onion, quartered
2 garlic cloves
5 cm/2 inch piece fresh root ginger, peeled
350 ml/12 fl oz natural yogurt

Masala:
75 g/3 oz ghee or butter (see page 11)
1 onion, thinly sliced
1 garlic clove, thinly sliced
1½ teaspoons ground turmeric
1½ teaspoons chilli powder
1 teaspoon ground cinnamon
seeds of 20 cardamom pods
1 teaspoon ground coriander
2 teaspoons aniseeds

Place the chicken in a bowl and sprinkle with lemon juice, salt and pepper. Mix to coat the chicken thoroughly, then cover and set aside.

Place the onion, garlic and ginger in a liquidizer or food processor and chop finely. Add the yogurt and strain in the lemon juice from the chicken. Purée until blended, then pour over the chicken. Cover and marinate in the refrigerator for 24 hours.

Thread the chicken on to kebab skewers, reserving the marinade. Barbecue or grill as slowly as possible until just cooked through (it is important not to overcook the chicken), about 6–8 minutes. Remove the chicken from the skewers.

Meanwhile, make the masala: melt the ghee in a wok, add the onion and garlic and fry for 4–5 minutes until soft. Sprinkle in the turmeric, chilli and cinnamon, stir well and fry for 1 minute.

Add the cardamom, coriander and aniseeds and stir-fry for 2 minutes, then add the reserved yogurt marinade. Mix well and bring to the boil. Add the chicken and cook for 3 minutes. Serve hot.

Serves 4–6
Preparation time: 45 minutes, plus 24 hours marinating
Cooking time: about 20 minutes

Coriander Chicken Curry

- 1.5 KG/3 LB CHICKEN, SKINNED AND CUT INTO PIECES
- 75 G/3 OZ GHEE OR BUTTER (SEE PAGE 11)
- 1 LARGE ONION, CHOPPED
- 1 TABLESPOON GROUND CORIANDER
- 1 TABLESPOON GARAM MASALA (SEE PAGE 11)
- 1 TEASPOON CHILLI POWDER
- 8 TOMATOES, FINELY CHOPPED
- 1 TEASPOON GROUND TURMERIC
- SALT
- 2 TABLESPOONS CHOPPED FRESH CORIANDER LEAVES
- SPRIGS OF FRESH CORIANDER LEAVES, TO GARNISH

Using a sharp knife, make a few slanting cuts in each piece of chicken and set aside.

Heat the ghee or butter in a large wok or heavy-based frying pan and fry the onion until it is lightly browned.

Add the ground coriander, garam masala and chilli powder and fry for a few seconds, stirring constantly. Add the tomatoes and fry for 5–7 minutes.

Stir in 300 ml/½ pint water, the turmeric and salt to taste. Bring the sauce to the boil, then add the chicken pieces and coat thoroughly with the sauce. Lower the heat, then cover and simmer until the chicken is tender.

Add the fresh coriander, stir and cook for a further 5–7 minutes. Serve at once, garnished with coriander sprigs.

SERVES 4–6

PREPARATION TIME: 30 MINUTES

COOKING TIME: ABOUT 45 MINUTES

Indonesian Chicken

- 8 chicken pieces, skinned
- juice of 1 lemon
- 4 tablespoons desiccated coconut, soaked in 4 tablespoons hot water
- 2–4 fresh red chillies, chopped
- 4 small onions, quartered
- 2 garlic cloves, peeled
- 4 Brazil nuts, shelled
- 1 cm/½ inch piece fresh root ginger, peeled
- 1 teaspoon grated lemon rind
- 1 teaspoon shrimp paste
- 1 teaspoon sugar
- 1 teaspoon salt
- 3 tablespoons oil

Rub the chicken pieces with lemon juice and leave to marinate for 20 minutes.

Put all the remaining ingredients, except the oil in a liquidizer or food processor and work to a smooth paste. Heat the oil in a large wok or heavy-based frying pan and gently fry the paste, stirring, for 5 minutes.

Add the chicken pieces and fry for 5 minutes. Stir in 300 ml/½ pint water and cook, uncovered, for 30 minutes, or until the chicken is tender and the sauce is thick. Serve hot.

Serves 4

Preparartion time: 15 minutes, plus 20 minutes marinating

Cooking time: 40 minutes

MEAT

BALTIS

UNLIKE OTHER FOOD COOKED BALTI-STYLE, MEAT GENERALLY NEEDS LONGER, SLOWER COOKING IF IT IS TO BE TENDER. THE TENDERIZATION PROCESS MAY BEGIN WITH A MARINADE, OR BY PARTLY COOKING THE MEAT BEFORE IT IS FINISHED OFF IN THE BALTI PAN WITH A SPICY SAUCE. IN BALTI COOKING, MEAT IS USUALLY LAMB, BUT WESTERN COOKS CAN USE BEEF OR PORK TO CONJURE UP A DELICIOUS RANGE OF CURRIES.

Balti Lamb

50 G/2 OZ GHEE OR BUTTER
(SEE PAGE 11)
500 G/1 LB LEAN LAMB, CUBED
1 LARGE ONION, CHOPPED
1 GARLIC CLOVE, CRUSHED
2.5 CM/1 INCH PIECE FRESH ROOT GINGER, PEELED AND GRATED
½ TEASPOON GROUND TURMERIC
2 TEASPOONS GARAM MASALA
(SEE PAGE 11)
1 TEASPOON CHILLI POWDER
75 G/3 OZ TOMATO PURÉE
SEEDS FROM 3 CARDAMOM PODS, CRUSHED
1 TEASPOON SALT
JUICE OF ½ LEMON
2 TOMATOES, QUARTERED, TO GARNISH

Melt the ghee or butter in a wok and fry the lamb gently to seal the meat on all sides. Remove with a slotted spoon and set aside. Fry the onion with the garlic, ginger, turmeric, garam masala and chilli powder for 4 minutes.

Return the meat to the wok, together with the tomato purée, cardamom seeds and 150 ml/¼ pint water. Stir well, then cover the wok and simmer gently for about 30 minutes, stirring occasionally. Add a little more water if the sauce appears to be sticking to the bottom of the wok.

Add the salt and lemon juice, then simmer very slowly for another 15 minutes, or until the lamb is tender. Serve hot, garnished with tomato quarters.

SERVES 4
PREPARATION TIME: 15 MINUTES
COOKING TIME: 50 MINUTES

Balti Liver

2 tablespoons mustard oil
1 onion, sliced
1 teaspoon ground turmeric
1 teaspoon chilli powder
1 teaspoon pepper
1 teaspoon ground ginger
1 teaspoon salt
500 g/1 lb liver, cut into 5 mm/¼ inch thick slices
1 garlic clove, chopped
To garnish:
2 tomatoes, chopped
chopped fresh coriander

Heat the oil in a wok or heavy-based frying pan and fry the onion until it is soft.

Mix the turmeric, chilli powder, pepper, ginger and salt together and add a little water to make a smooth paste. Rub the spice paste into the liver.

Add the liver and chopped garlic to the wok and stir-fry for about 5–10 minutes, or until the liver is tender.

Serve at once, garnished with chopped tomatoes and coriander.

Serves 4
Preparation time: 10 minutes
Cooking time: about 10 minutes

Balti Keema

2 TABLESPOONS VEGETABLE OIL
500 G/1 LB GREEN PEPPERS, DESEEDED AND SLICED
500 G/1 LB ONIONS, SLICED
2 TEASPOONS SALT
2 TEASPOONS PEPPER
½ TEASPOON GROUND CUMIN
2 TEASPOONS GARAM MASALA (SEE PAGE 11)
PINCH OF GROUND CINNAMON
1½ TEASPOONS CHILLI POWDER
750 G/1½ LB MINCED LAMB
2 TOMATOES, QUARTERED, TO GARNISH

Heat the oil in a wok or heavy-based frying pan and stir-fry the peppers for about 1 minute. Remove the peppers with a slotted spoon and keep warm.

Add the onions to the oil and fry until they are golden brown. Add the salt, pepper, cumin, garam masala, cinnamon and chilli powder and stir-fry for 2 minutes.

Add the minced lamb and cook gently for about 20 minutes, stirring frequently to make sure that it does not stick to the bottom of the wok.

Return the green peppers to the wok and heat through over a low heat for a further 10 minutes. Serve garnished with the tomatoes.

SERVES 4–6
PREPARATION TIME: 15 MINUTES
COOKING TIME: 35 MINUTES

Balti Lamb Madras

- 1 TABLESPOON MUSTARD OIL
- 1 ONION, CHOPPED
- 2 GARLIC CLOVES, CRUSHED
- 2 FRESH GREEN CHILLIES, DESEEDED AND SLICED
- 2 TEASPOONS CHILLI POWDER
- 2 TEASPOONS GARAM MASALA (SEE PAGE 11)
- 500 G/1 LB LEAN LAMB, CUT INTO 4 CM/1½ INCH CUBES
- 1 TABLESPOON VINEGAR
- 1 TEASPOON SALT
- 2 TOMATOES, SKINNED, DESEEDED AND CHOPPED
- 1 TABLESPOON COCONUT FLAKES

Heat the oil in a wok or heavy-based frying pan and stir-fry the onion, garlic, chillies and chilli powder for 2 minutes. Add the garam masala, the cubes of lamb, the vinegar, salt and chopped tomatoes. Stir the mixture thoroughly.

Cover the wok, and cook for 30–40 minutes over a moderate heat until the lamb is tender, adding a little water if it appears to be sticking to the bottom of the wok.

Transfer to a heated serving dish, scatter the coconut flakes over and serve immediately.

SERVES 4

PREPARATION TIME: 10 MINUTES

COOKING TIME: 35–45 MINUTES

Balti Lamb with Tomatoes

- 4 tablespoons vegetable oil
- 1 onion, chopped
- 25 g/1 oz fresh root ginger, peeled and grated
- 4–5 garlic cloves, crushed
- ½ teaspoon ground turmeric
- 1 teaspoon ground coriander
- 1½ teaspoons ground cumin
- 500 g/1 lb boned leg of lamb, cubed
- 1–2 fresh green chillies, deseeded and very finely chopped, or 1 teaspoon chilli powder
- 425 g/14 oz can chopped tomatoes
- 2–3 sprigs of fresh coriander leaves, chopped, plus extra to garnish
- 1 teaspoon salt

Heat the oil in a large wok or heavy-based saucepan and fry the onion until lightly browned. Add the ginger, garlic, turmeric, coriander, cumin and the lamb. Mix together well, then cover and cook over a gentle heat for 10–12 minutes.

Add the chillies or chilli powder, the chopped tomatoes, coriander leaves and salt. Cover the wok and cook for a further 50 minutes, or until the lamb is tender. Serve hot, garnished with chopped coriander.

Serves 4

Preparation time: 20 minutes

Cooking time: 1 hour 10 minutes

Lamb Dopiaza

125 g/4 oz ghee or butter (see page 11)
500 g/1 lb onions, sliced
500 g/1 lb boned shoulder of lamb, cut into 2.5 cm/1 inch cubes
1 teaspoon chilli powder
½ teaspoon ground ginger
1 teaspoon salt
300 ml/½ pint natural yogurt
2 garlic cloves, crushed
4 cardamom seeds
1 teaspoon garam masala (see page 11)
½ teaspoon cumin seeds, dry-roasted and ground

Melt the ghee or butter in a wok or heavy-based frying pan and fry half the onions over a very low heat, until soft and golden brown. Remove from the wok with a slotted spoon and set aside.

Increase the heat and sauté the meat until it is sealed on all sides. Remove the meat from the wok and set aside.

Add the chilli powder, ginger, salt and the remaining onions, then stir in the yogurt. Cook for 2 minutes, then return the meat to the wok. Cover and simmer for 10 minutes.

Add the garlic, cardamom seeds, garam masala, cumin seeds and the browned onions. Cover and simmer for 30 minutes, or until the lamb is tender, adding a little water if necessary to prevent it from sticking to the bottom of the wok. Serve hot.

Serves 4
Preparation time: 15 minutes
Cooking time: 45–50 minutes

Lamb Korma

½ TEASPOON SAFFRON THREADS
50 G/2 OZ UNSALTED CASHEW NUTS
3 FRESH GREEN CHILLIES, DESEEDED
25 G/1 OZ FRESH ROOT GINGER, PEELED AND CHOPPED
2.5 CM/1 INCH PIECE CINNAMON STICK
½ TEASPOON CARDAMOM SEEDS
6 CLOVES
3 GARLIC CLOVES
2 TEASPOONS GROUND CORIANDER
½ TEASPOON CUMIN SEEDS
50 G/2 OZ GHEE OR BUTTER (SEE PAGE 11)
1 LARGE ONION, SLICED
1 TEASPOON SALT
300 ML/½ PINT NATURAL YOGURT
500 G/1 LB BONED LEG OR SHOULDER OF LAMB, CUBED
1 TABLESPOON FRESH CORIANDER, CHOPPED, PLUS EXTRA TO GARNISH
2 TEASPOONS LEMON JUICE

Put the saffron in a small bowl and pour in 3–4 tablespoons boiling water. Infuse for 10 minutes.

Place the cashew nuts, chillies, ginger, cinnamon, cardamom seeds, cloves, garlic, coriander and cumin seeds in a liquidizer together with 300 ml/½ pint water and blend for 2 minutes to form a smooth purée.

Heat the ghee or butter in a wok until very hot and fry the onion until golden brown. Stir in the salt, spice purée and the yogurt. Cook gently for 5 minutes, stirring occasionally.

Add the lamb and stir well, coating the lamb with the mixture. Cover and cook over a low heat for 20 minutes, stirring occasionally.

Add the saffron, together with its soaking water, and the fresh coriander, and cook for another 10 minutes, or until the lamb is tender. Sprinkle with lemon juice, and serve at once garnished with chopped coriander.

SERVES 4
PREPARATION TIME: 15 MINUTES
COOKING TIME: 30–35 MINUTES

Mogul-style Lamb

2 TEASPOONS CUMIN SEEDS
1 TABLESPOON CORIANDER SEEDS
300 ML/½ PINT NATURAL YOGURT
1 TEASPOON GROUND TURMERIC
½ TEASPOON PEPPER
500 G/1 LB BONED LEG OR SHOULDER OF LAMB, CUT INTO 1 CM/½ INCH CUBES
40 G/1½ OZ GHEE OR BUTTER (SEE PAGE 11)
1 ONION, FINELY CHOPPED
2 GARLIC CLOVES, CRUSHED
2.5 CM/1 INCH PIECE FRESH ROOT GINGER, PEELED AND FINELY CHOPPED
½ TEASPOON GROUND CLOVES
1 TEASPOON GROUND CARDAMOM
3 TABLESPOONS GROUND ALMONDS
150 ML/¼ PINT DOUBLE CREAM
½ TEASPOON SALT
2–3 TEASPOONS LEMON JUICE
TO GARNISH:
1 TABLESPOON FLAKED ALMONDS
1 LEMON, QUARTERED

Put the cumin and coriander seeds in a small saucepan and heat gently for 1 minute to release the aromatic oils. Grind the seeds in a spice mill or a mortar and pestle.

Put the yogurt in a bowl and stir in the cumin and coriander with the turmeric and pepper. Mix in the lamb, cover and refrigerate for 2 hours.

Melt the ghee or butter in a large wok or heavy-based saucepan, add the onion and fry for 5 minutes until soft but not browned. Add the garlic, ginger, cloves and cardamom and fry for 4 minutes more.

Add the lamb with the marinade and ground almonds. Bring to the boil and boil briskly for a few minutes, then cover and simmer gently for 1½ hours, or until the lamb is tender. Stir occasionally adding water if necessary.

Stir in the cream, add salt and lemon juice to taste and simmer for 2–3 minutes until heated through. Transfer to a heated serving dish, scatter with almonds and garnish with lemon wedges.

SERVES 4

PREPARATION TIME: 5 MINUTES, PLUS 2 HOURS MARINATING

COOKING TIME: ABOUT 1½ HOURS

Rogan Josh (Lamb with Tomatoes and Almonds)

- 50 G/2 OZ GHEE OR BUTTER (SEE PAGE 11)
- 1 ONION, FINELY CHOPPED
- 5 SMALL GREEN CARDAMOM PODS
- ½ TEASPOON GROUND TURMERIC
- 1 TEASPOON CHILLI POWDER
- 1 TEASPOON GROUND CUMIN
- 1½ TEASPOONS PAPRIKA
- 1 TEASPOON GROUND CORIANDER
- 150 ML/¼ PINT NATURAL YOGURT
- 250 G/8 OZ CAN TOMATOES, FINELY CHOPPED
- 500 G/1 LB BONED LEG OF LAMB, CUT INTO 2.5 CM/1 INCH CUBES
- 1 TEASPOON SALT
- CHOPPED FRESH CORIANDER LEAVES, TO GARNISH

MASALA:

- 15 G/½ OZ FRESH ROOT GINGER, PEELED
- 6–7 GARLIC CLOVES
- 1 BLADE OF MACE
- ¼ TEASPOON GROUND NUTMEG
- 4 CLOVES
- 12 PEPPERCORNS
- 50 G/2 OZ ALMONDS, BLANCHED
- 2 LARGE CARDAMOM PODS
- A PINCH OF SAFFRON THREADS
- 1 TABLESPOON POPPY SEEDS, DRY-ROASTED (OPTIONAL)

First make the masala: grind the ginger, garlic, mace, nutmeg, cloves, peppercorns, almonds, cardamoms, saffron and poppy seeds, if using, with a little water to make a fine paste.

Heat the ghee or butter in a wok and fry the onion until browned. Add the cardamoms and stir in the spice paste. Fry for 2 minutes, taking care not to burn the mixture. Add the turmeric, chilli powder, cumin, paprika and coriander and fry for 2 minutes more. Stir in the yogurt and tomatoes. Stir in the lamb and a little salt.

Cover and cook over a gentle heat for 40–50 minutes, sprinkling with a little water if necessary. Serve garnished with chopped coriander leaves.

SERVES 4

PREPARATION TIME: 30 MINUTES

COOKING TIME: 1 HOUR 10 MINUTES

Lamb in Coconut Cream

500 G/1 LB BONED LEG OF LAMB, CUT INTO 2.5 CM/1 INCH CUBES
1 TEASPOON SALT
1 TEASPOON GROUND TURMERIC
1 TEASPOON CHILLI POWDER
2 TEASPOONS GROUND CINNAMON
1 LARGE ONION, FINELY CHOPPED
2 GARLIC CLOVES, CRUSHED
50 G/2 OZ PIECE FRESH ROOT GINGER, PEELED AND CHOPPED
125 G/4 OZ CREAMED COCONUT, GRATED
150 ML/¼ PINT DOUBLE CREAM
150 ML/¼ PINT NATURAL YOGURT
CHOPPED FRESH CORIANDER, TO GARNISH

Place the lamb, salt, spices, onion, garlic, ginger and 450 ml/¾ pint water in a large wok or frying pan and bring to the boil, stirring occasionally. Skim if necessary.

Cover and simmer, stirring occasionally, for about 1¼ hours, or until the lamb is tender. Remove the lid for the last 15 minutes of cooking so that most of the liquid can evaporate.

Remove the wok from the heat and add the creamed coconut, cream and yogurt. Stir constantly until the coconut has melted.

Heat gently for 10–15 minutes: the sauce should thicken but should not boil. Serve hot, sprinkled with chopped coriander.

SERVES 4
PREPARATION TIME: 20 MINUTES
COOKING TIME: 1½ HOURS

Lamb and Potato with Fenugreek

2 ONIONS, SLICED
6 TABLESPOONS VEGETABLE OIL
2 LARGE GARLIC CLOVES, CRUSHED
2.5 CM/1 INCH PIECE FRESH ROOT GINGER, PEELED AND GRATED
1 TEASPOON GROUND TURMERIC
4 FRESH GREEN CHILLIES, CHOPPED
750 G/1½ LB SHOULDER OF LAMB, CUT INTO SMALL PIECES (WITH THE BONE)
1½ TEASPOONS SALT
6 TABLESPOONS CHOPPED FRESH FENUGREEK LEAVES
4 POTATOES, DICED

Fry the onions in the oil until golden. Add the garlic, ginger, turmeric and 2 of the chillies and stir-fry for 2–3 minutes. Add the meat and continue to stir-fry for a few minutes to seal the meat on all sides.

Add 450 ml/¾ pint water and the salt, then bring to the boil. Lower the heat, cover the wok and simmer for about 30–40 minutes, or until the lamb is tender.

Add the fenugreek leaves and the diced potatoes and cook for a further 15 minutes, or until the potatoes are tender. Sprinkle the remaining chopped chillies over the lamb and potatoes, cover the wok and leave over a low heat for a few minutes. Serve hot.

SERVES 4–6
PREPARATION TIME: 20 MINUTES
COOKING TIME: ABOUT 1 HOUR

Lamb and Chickpea Curry

40 g/1½ oz dried tamarind, soaked in 200 ml/7 fl oz boiling water for 30 minutes
2–3 tablespoons vegetable oil
1 onion, finely chopped
2.5 cm/1 inch piece cinnamon stick
1 garlic clove, crushed
1 teaspoon ground ginger
375 g/12 oz shoulder or breast of lamb, trimmed and chopped into pieces (with the bone)
1 teaspoon chilli powder
1 teaspoon ground cumin
½ teaspoon ground turmeric
2–3 tomatoes, skinned and sliced
8–10 curry leaves
425 g/14 oz can chickpeas, drained and roughly mashed
200–250 g/7–8 oz marrow, peeled, deseeded and sliced, or courgettes, sliced
salt
To garnish:
1 fresh green chilli, deseeded and very finely chopped
2–3 sprigs of fresh coriander leaves, chopped

Strain the tamarind liquid through a wire sieve set over a small bowl, pressing to extract as much pulp as possible. Repeat this process to extract any remaining pulp.

Heat the oil in a large wok or heavy-based saucepan and fry the onion until lightly browned. Add the cinnamon, garlic, ginger and the lamb and fry for 4–5 minutes. Stir in the chilli powder, cumin, turmeric and tomatoes, and stir-fry for a few minutes. Add the tamarind pulp, curry leaves, 570 ml/1¼ pints water, and a pinch of salt. Cover and gently simmer for 50–60 minutes, or until the lamb is cooked.

Stir in the mashed chickpeas and the marrow or courgette slices, and continue simmering until tender and the sauce is fairly thick. Serve hot, garnished with the chopped chilli and coriander leaves.

Serves 4
Preparation time: 50 minutes
Cooking time: 1½–1¾ hours

Balti Beef

4 TABLESPOONS VEGETABLE OIL
1 LARGE ONION, CHOPPED
½ TEASPOON GROUND CORIANDER
½ TEASPOON GROUND TURMERIC
2.5 CM/1 INCH PIECE FRESH ROOT GINGER, FINELY CHOPPED
1 GARLIC CLOVE, CRUSHED
1 FRESH RED OR GREEN CHILLI, CHOPPED
500 G/1 LB FRYING STEAK, CUT INTO STRIPS ABOUT 2.5 X 4 CM/1 X 1½ INCHES
1 GREEN OR RED PEPPER, DESEEDED AND ROUGHLY CHOPPED
2 TOMATOES, QUARTERED
JUICE OF 1 LEMON
SALT

Heat the oil in a wok or heavy-based frying pan, add the onion and fry until soft. Add the coriander, turmeric, ginger, garlic and chilli and stir-fry over a low heat for 5 minutes; if the mixture becomes dry, add 1 tablespoon of water.

Add the steak, increase the heat and stir-fry until browned all over. Add the chopped pepper, then cover and cook over a low heat for 5–10 minutes, stirring occasionally, until the meat is tender. Add the tomatoes, lemon juice and salt to taste and cook, uncovered, for 2–3 minutes. Serve hot.

SERVES 4
PREPARATION TIME: 15 MINUTES
COOKING TIME: 15–20 MINUTES

Balti Beef and Broccoli

50 g/2 oz ghee or butter (see page 11)
1 large onion, chopped
2 garlic cloves, crushed
500 g/1 lb frying steak, cut into narrow strips
1 tablespoon ground coriander
1 teaspoon garam masala (see page 11)
1 teaspoon chilli powder
1 teaspoon mustard powder
250 g/8 oz can tomatoes, chopped wit the juice
250 g/8 oz broccoli, washed and separated into florets, stalks sliced
salt

Melt the ghee or butter in a wok or heavy-based frying pan and fry the onion until it is lightly browned. Add the garlic and fry for a further minute.

Add the steak, increase the heat and stir-fry until the steak is browned on all sides. Lower the heat, then cover and cook the meat in its own juices until tender, about 10 minutes.

Add the coriander, garam masala, chilli, mustard and a pinch of salt and stir-fry over a low heat for a few seconds. Stir in the tomatoes and cook, uncovered, until almost dry. Add the broccoli and stir-fry for a few minutes. Partly cover the wok and simmer until tender, then serve at once.

Serves 4
Preparation time: 20 minutes
Cooking time: 30 minutes

Calcutta Beef Curry

- 1 TEASPOON SALT
- 1 TABLESPOON CHILLI POWDER
- 2 TEASPOONS GROUND CORIANDER
- 1 TEASPOON PEPPER
- 1½ TEASPOONS GROUND TURMERIC
- 1 TEASPOON GROUND CUMIN
- 1 LITRE/1¾ PINTS MILK
- 1–1.2 KG/2–2½ LB BRAISING STEAK, TRIMMED AND CUT INTO 4 CM/1½ INCH CUBES
- 50 G/2 OZ GHEE OR BUTTER (SEE PAGE 11)
- 2 LARGE ONIONS, THINLY SLICED
- 5 GARLIC CLOVES, THINLY SLICED
- 7 CM/3 INCH PIECE FRESH ROOT GINGER, PEELED AND THINLY SLICED
- 2 TEASPOONS GARAM MASALA (SEE PAGE 11)

Put the salt and the ground spices, except the garam masala, into a large bowl. Mix in a little of the milk to make a paste, then gradually stir in the remaining milk. Add the beef cubes and mix in the milk and spice mixture until they are evenly coated.

Melt the ghee or butter in a wok or heavy-based saucepan, add the onions, garlic and ginger and fry gently for 4–5 minutes, until soft. Remove the beef cubes from the milk and spice mixture with a slotted spoon, add to the wok and stir-fry over a moderate heat until browned on all sides.

Increase the heat, add the milk and spice mixture and bring to the boil. Cover the wok, lower the heat and cook gently for 1½–2 hours, or until the beef is tender and the sauce reduced.

Just before serving, sprinkle in the garam masala. Increase the heat and boil off any excess liquid so that you are left with a thick sauce. Transfer to a warmed serving dish and serve immediately.

SERVES 4–6

PREPARATION TIME: 15 MINUTES

COOKING TIME: ABOUT 2 HOURS

Beef and Potato Curry

4 tablespoons vegetable oil
2 onions, finely chopped
2 garlic cloves, chopped
1 teaspoon chilli powder
1 tablespoon ground cumin seeds
1½ tablespoons ground coriander
2.5 cm/1 inch piece fresh root ginger, finely chopped
750 g/1½ lb braising steak, cubed
2 tablespoons tomato purée
375 g/12 oz small new potatoes
4 fresh green chillies
salt

Heat the oil in a large wok or heavy-based saucepan, add the onions and fry until lightly browned. Add the garlic, chilli powder, cumin, coriander and ginger and cook gently for 5 minutes, stirring occasionally; if the mixture becomes dry, add 2 tablespoons of water.

Add the beef and cook, stirring, until the meat is browned all over. Add the tomato purée, salt to taste and just enough water to cover the meat; stir thoroughly. Bring to the boil, then cover, lower the heat and simmer for about 1 hour, or until the meat is almost tender. Add the potatoes and whole chillies and simmer until the potatoes are cooked. Serve hot.

Serves 4
Preparation time: 15 minutes
Cooking time: about 1½ hours

Balti Minced Beef

4 TABLESPOONS VEGETABLE OIL
2 ONIONS, FINELY CHOPPED
2 TEASPOONS GROUND CORIANDER
½ TEASPOON GROUND CUMIN SEEDS
½ TEASPOON GROUND TURMERIC
2.5 CM/1 INCH PIECE FRESH ROOT GINGER, FINELY CHOPPED
1 FRESH GREEN CHILLI, FINELY CHOPPED
1 HEAPED TEASPOON GARAM MASALA (SEE PAGE 11)
500 G/1 LB MINCED BEEF
250 G/8 OZ SMALL POTATOES, QUARTERED
500 G/1 LB SHELLED PEAS
SALT

Heat the oil in a wok or heavy-based frying pan, add the onions and cook until soft. Add the spices and fry for 5 minutes over a low heat; if the mixture becomes dry, add 1 tablespoon of water.

Stir in the minced beef and cook over a high heat until the meat is evenly browned.

Lower the heat and add the potatoes and salt to taste. Cover and cook gently for 10 minutes, then add the peas. Continue cooking until the potatoes and peas are tender. Serve hot.

SERVES 4
PREPARATION TIME: 15 MINUTES
COOKING TIME: 20–25 MINUTES

Masala Mince

- 1 tablespoon chopped fresh coriander, plus extra to garnish
- 1 teaspoon chopped fresh mint
- 3 fresh green chillies, chopped
- 3 tablespoons natural yogurt
- 500 g/1 lb lean minced beef
- 1 onion, sliced
- 50 g/2 oz lentils, washed and soaked for 3 hours
- 4 tablespoons vegetable oil
- 1 large garlic clove, crushed
- 1 cm/½ inch piece fresh root ginger, grated
- ½ teaspoon ground turmeric
- 2 cloves
- 4 cardamoms
- 2.5 cm/1 inch piece cinnamon stick
- 1½ teaspoons salt

Mix the coriander, mint and 2 of the chillies with the yogurt and set aside. Place all the other ingredients except the salt in a wok or heavy-based saucepan. Add just enough water to cover the mixture, bring to the boil, cover and cook over a medium heat for 20 minutes or until the lentils are almost cooked.

Remove the lid, raise the heat slightly and add the yogurt mixture and salt, stirring constantly. The mince should separate and the oil should come to the surface. Serve immediately, garnished with chopped fresh coriander.

Serves 4

Preparation time: 15 minutes

Cooking time: 30 minutes

Kofta Curry

3 TABLESPOONS VEGETABLE OIL
2.5 CM/1 INCH PIECE CINNAMON STICK
10 CLOVES
1 ONION, CHOPPED
2 GARLIC CLOVES, FINELY CHOPPED
5 CM/2 INCH PIECE FRESH ROOT GINGER, CHOPPED
1 TABLESPOON GROUND CUMIN SEEDS
2 TABLESPOONS GROUND CORIANDER
1 TEASPOON CHILLI POWDER
425 G/14 OZ CAN CHOPPED TOMATOES, WITH THE JUICE
750 G/1½ LB MINCED BEEF
2 FRESH GREEN CHILLIES, FINELY CHOPPED
3 TABLESPOONS FINELY CHOPPED FRESH CORIANDER
1 TEASPOON GARAM MASALA (SEE PAGE 11)
1 EGG, LIGHTLY BEATEN
SALT

Heat the oil in a large wok or heavy-based frying pan. Add the cinnamon and cloves and fry for 30 seconds, then add the onion and fry until golden, stirring occasionally.

Add the garlic, ginger, cumin, coriander, chilli powder and salt to taste. Stir well and fry over a low heat for 2 minutes, adding 1–2 tablespoons of water if the mixture begins to stick. Add the tomatoes with their juice and stir well. Cover and leave to simmer while preparing the kofta (meatballs).

Mix together the beef, chillies, fresh coriander, garam masala and egg, adding salt to taste. With dampened hands, shape the mixture into about 40 walnut-sized balls. Slip them into the sauce in a single layer and simmer very gently for about 30 minutes, turning the meatballs over very carefully every 10 minutes. Serve hot.

SERVES 4–6
PREPARATION TIME: 30 MINUTES
COOKING TIME: ABOUT 45 MINUTES

Pork with Tamarind

50 G/2 OZ DRIED TAMARIND
75 G/3 OZ GHEE OR BUTTER (SEE PAGE 11)
2 LARGE ONIONS, SLICED
8 GARLIC CLOVES, SLICED
750 G/1½ LB LEAN PORK, CUBED
½ TEASPOON PAPRIKA
½ TEASPOON GROUND TURMERIC
1 TEASPOON FENUGREEK SEEDS
25 G/1 OZ FRESH ROOT GINGER, PEELED AND CHOPPED
2 FRESH GREEN CHILLIES
1 TEASPOON SALT
1½ TEASPOONS GARAM MASALA (SEE PAGE 11)
2 BAY LEAVES
6 CARDAMOMS
3 CLOVES
FRESH CORIANDER LEAVES, TO GARNISH

Put the tamarind in a bowl and pour over 300 ml/½ pint boiling water. Leave to soak for 30 minutes.

Melt the ghee or butter in a wok or heavy-based frying pan and fry the onions and garlic until soft, then add the pork and stir-fry to seal the meat on all sides.

Add the paprika, turmeric, fenugreek, ginger, chillies and salt. Add 150 ml/¼ pint water, cover and cook for 20–30 minutes.

Mash the tamarind in the soaking water, then strain through a wire sieve set over a bowl, pressing the tamarind to extract as much pulp as possible.

Uncover the wok and bring to the boil until nearly all the liquid has evaporated. Add the rest of the spices and the tamarind pulp and cook over a very low heat for about 30 minutes, or until the pork is tender. Serve hot, garnished with coriander.

SERVES 4–6
PREPARATION TIME: 20 MINUTES

Pork with Pineapple

50 G/2 OZ GHEE OR BUTTER (SEE PAGE 11)
1 LARGE ONION, FINELY CHOPPED
1½ TEASPOONS GARAM MASALA (SEE PAGE 11)
1½ TEASPOONS GROUND CINNAMON
1½ TEASPOONS GROUND GINGER
1½ TEASPOONS CHILLI POWDER
1½ TEASPOONS GARLIC POWDER
425 G/14 OZ CAN CHOPPED TOMATOES
1 PINEAPPLE, CUBED
750 G/1½ LB PORK STEAK, CUT INTO 2.5–4 CM/1–1½ INCH PIECES AND TRIMMED
SALT

Heat the ghee or butter in a large wok or heavy-based saucepan and fry the onion until it is soft and translucent.

Stir in the spices and garlic powder and fry for a few seconds, then add the tomatoes and simmer for 5–7 minutes.

Add 150 ml/¼ pint water, the cubed pineapple, the pork and salt, stir well, then cover and cook over a gentle heat for about 1 hour, until the pork is tender. Stir occasionally during the cooking time. Serve hot.

SERVES 4–6
PREPARATION TIME: 25 MINUTES
COOKING TIME: ABOUT 1 HOUR

Pork Vindaloo

125 ML/4 FL OZ VINEGAR
750 G/1½ LB LEAN PORK, CUBED
1 LARGE ONION, ROUGHLY CHOPPED
1 TEASPOON CUMIN SEEDS
2 TEASPOONS MUSTARD SEEDS
5–6 GARLIC CLOVES, PEELED AND CRUSHED
15 G/½ OZ FRESH ROOT GINGER, PEELED, OR ½ TEASPOON GROUND GINGER
4 CLOVES
2.5 CM/1 INCH PIECE CINNAMON STICK
6–8 PEPPERCORNS
40 G/1½ OZ GHEE OR 3 TABLESPOONS OIL (SEE PAGE 11)
6–8 CURRY LEAVES
500 G/1 LB TOMATOES, SKINNED AND CHOPPED
½ TEASPOON GROUND TURMERIC
SALT
2–3 SPRIGS OF FRESH CORIANDER LEAVES, CHOPPED, TO GARNISH

Blend 1 tablespoon of the vinegar with a little water and rinse the pork in this mixture. Drain and pat dry with kitchen paper.

Put the onion, cumin seeds, mustard seeds, garlic, ginger, cloves, cinnamon and peppercorns into a liquidizer or food processor with a little of the remaining vinegar and purée to a thick paste. Place the pork into a large bowl, add the paste and mix thoroughly. Cover and set aside to marinate for 15–20 minutes.

Heat the ghee or oil in a wok or frying pan and fry the curry leaves until golden brown. Add the marinated pork, tomatoes and turmeric, and keep stirring until the tomatoes are broken up. Add any remaining vinegar and a pinch of salt. Cover and simmer for about 40–50 minutes, until the pork is tender. A little water may be added during cooking if necessary, although the sauce should be fairly thick. Serve hot, garnished with coriander leaves.

SERVES 4–6
PREPARATION TIME: 30 MINUTES, PLUS 15–20 MINUTES MARINATING
COOKING TIME: ABOUT 1 HOUR

VEGETABLES

AND PULSES

BALTI COOKING IS A VEGETARIAN'S DREAM – THE APPETIZING VARIETY OF COLOURS, FLAVOURS AND TEXTURES MAKES IT EASY TO CREATE A BALANCED MENU FROM TWO OR THREE DISHES. OF COURSE, YOU DO NOT HAVE TO BE VEGETARIAN TO ENJOY THESE HEALTHY, QUICKLY COOKED, SPICY VEGETABLES – AND DO NOT WORRY IF ANY OF THE INGREDIENTS ARE UNAVAILABLE: SIMPLY USE WHATEVER IS IN SEASON.

Balti Mixed Vegetables

- 2–3 tablespoons vegetable oil
- 1 small onion, chopped
- 1 garlic clove, crushed
- 2.5 cm/1 inch piece fresh root ginger, grated
- 1 teaspoon chilli powder
- 2 teaspoons ground coriander
- ½ teaspoon ground turmeric
- 500 g/1 lb diced mixed vegetables (e.g. potatoes, carrots, swede, peas, beans, cauliflower)
- 2–3 tomatoes, skinned and chopped, or juice of 1 lemon
- salt

Heat the oil in a large wok or heavy-based saucepan and gently fry the onion for 5–10 minutes, or until lightly browned. Add the garlic, ginger, chilli powder, coriander, turmeric and a pinch of salt. Fry for 2–3 minutes, then add the diced vegetables and stir-fry for a further 2–3 minutes.

Add either the chopped tomatoes or the lemon juice. Stir well and add a little water. Cover and cook gently for 10–12 minutes, or until the vegetables are tender, adding a little more water if necessary to prevent the vegetables from sticking to the bottom of the wok.

Serve at once with chapatis or naan.

Serves 4

Preparation time: 15 minutes

Cooking time: 20–30 minutes

Balti Vegetable Korma

1 small cauliflower, cut into florets
175 g/6 oz carrots, diced
175 g/6 oz potatoes, diced
250 g/8 oz broad beans or green beans, cut into 2.5 cm/1 inch pieces
40 g/1½ oz ghee or butter (see page 11)
1 large onion, sliced
1 tablespoon curry powder
1 teaspoon curry paste
1 tablespoon plain flour
2 tablespoons mango chutney
150 ml/¼ pint single cream
2 tablespoons blanched almonds
salt
To garnish:
4 hard-boiled eggs, cut into wedges
a pinch of paprika

Steam the cauliflower, carrots and potatoes over boiling salted water for 10 minutes. Cook the beans in boiling, salted water for 5 minutes.

Drain the vegetables, reserving the cooking liquid from the beans, and keep them warm.

Heat the ghee or butter in a large wok or heavy-based saucepan and gently fry the onion for 5 minutes, until soft. Add the curry powder, increase the heat to moderate and stir-fry for 1 minute. Stir in the curry paste and flour and cook for 1 minute, then add the mango chutney.

Measure 600 ml/1 pint of the vegetable cooking liquid, or make it up to that amount with water or vegetable stock. Pour the stock gradually on to the curry mixture, stirring, and bring to the boil. Simmer for 5 minutes, then stir in the vegetables and allow them just to heat through. Stir in the cream and almonds.

Serve hot, garnished with the eggs and a light dusting of paprika.

Serves 4
Preparation time: 15 minutes
Cooking time: 35 minutes

Mixed Vegetable Curry

3 tablespoons vegetable oil
1 teaspoon fennel seeds
2 onions, sliced
1 teaspoon ground coriander
1 teaspoon cumin seeds
1 teaspoon chilli powder
2 teaspoons chopped fresh root ginger
2 garlic cloves, crushed
1 small aubergine, thinly sliced
1 potato, cubed
1 green pepper, deseeded and sliced
2 courgettes, sliced
425 g/14 oz can chopped tomatoes
2 fresh green chillies, deseeded and chopped
50 g/2 oz frozen peas
salt

Heat the oil in a large wok or heavy-based saucepan, stir in the fennel seeds and cook for 1 minute, stirring constantly. Add the onions and cook for 5 minutes, until lightly browned. Lower the heat, add all the dry spices and stir-fry for 1 minute. Add the ginger, garlic, aubergine and potato, mix well and cook for 15 minutes.

Add the green pepper, courgettes, tomatoes with their juice, chillies and salt to taste. Bring slowly to the boil, then simmer, stirring occasionally, for 10 minutes.

Stir in the peas and cook for 3 minutes. Transfer the curry to a warmed serving dish and serve at once with naan.

Serves 4–6
Preparation time: 15 minutes
Cooking time: about 40 minutes

Braised Okra with Chillies

- 50 G/2 OZ GHEE OR BUTTER (SEE PAGE 11)
- 1 LARGE ONION, SLICED
- 3 GARLIC CLOVES, SLICED
- 5 CM/2 INCH PIECE FRESH ROOT GINGER, PEELED AND FINELY CHOPPED
- 2 FRESH GREEN CHILLIES, DESEEDED AND FINELY CHOPPED
- ½ TEASPOON CHILLI POWDER
- 500 G/1 LB OKRA, TOPPED AND TAILED
- 2 TEASPOONS DESICCATED COCONUT
- SALT

Melt the ghee or butter in a large wok or heavy-based saucepan, add the onion, garlic, ginger, chillies and chilli powder and fry gently for 4–5 minutes until soft, stirring occasionally.

Add the okra, 200 ml/7 fl oz water and salt to taste. Bring to the boil, then lower the heat, cover and simmer for 5–10 minutes, until the okra are just tender, but still firm to the bite. Stir in the coconut and serve hot.

SERVES 4

PREPARATION TIME: 15 MINUTES

COOKING TIME: ABOUT 15 MINUTES

Peas with Indian Cheese

125 g/4 oz ghee or butter (see page 11)
About 125 g/4 oz paneer (Indian curd cheese), cubed; alternatively use beancurd or feta cheese
1 onion, sliced
1 teaspoon ground ginger
½ teaspoon ground cumin
½ teaspoon chilli powder
½ teaspoon salt
500 g/1 lb frozen peas
2 tomatoes, chopped

Melt the ghee or butter in a large wok or heavy-based frying pan, add the cubed cheese and fry until it is browned on all sides. Remove the cheese with a slotted spoon, drain on kitchen paper and set aside.

Add the onion to the wok and fry gently for about 4–5 minutes, until soft. Add the spices and salt and stir-fry for 3 minutes more.

Add the peas and tomatoes and stir gently until the peas are coated with the spice mixture. Stir in the reserved cheese and heat through, taking care not to break up the cubes of cheese. Serve hot.

Serves 4
Preparation time: 5 minutes
Cooking time: 10–15 minutes

Aviyal

125 G/4 OZ GHEE OR BUTTER (SEE PAGE 11)
25 G/1 OZ FRESH ROOT GINGER, PEELED AND CHOPPED
3 GARLIC CLOVES, CHOPPED
½ TEASPOON MUSTARD SEEDS
1 LARGE ONION, CHOPPED
2 TEASPOONS GROUND CORIANDER
3 TEASPOONS GARAM MASALA (SEE PAGE 11)
1 TEASPOON GROUND TURMERIC
2 TEASPOONS SALT
250 G/8 OZ BROCCOLI OR KALE, CUT INTO 2.5 CM/1 INCH PIECES
2 RED PEPPERS, DESEEDED AND CUT INTO 2.5 CM/1 INCH SQUARES
175 G/6 OZ CARROTS, SLICED
125 G/4 OZ RUNNER BEANS, CUT INTO 2.5 CM/1 INCH PIECES
400 ML/14 FL OZ COCONUT MILK
1 FRESH GREEN CHILLI, DESEEDED AND FINELY CHOPPED
125 G/4 OZ FRESH CORIANDER, TO GARNISH

Heat the ghee or butter in a large wok and add the ginger, garlic and mustard seeds and fry for about 1 minute. Add the onion and fry gently until golden brown.

Add the coriander, garam masala, turmeric and salt and simmer for a further 5 minutes.

Add the vegetables and stir gently for about 5 minutes, then stir in the coconut milk and the green chilli. Bring to the boil and simmer, covered, for about 15 minutes.

Serve hot, sprinkled with the chopped coriander.

SERVES 4
PREPARATION TIME: ABOUT 25 MINUTES
COOKING TIME: 30 MINUTES

Hyderabadi Aubergines

VEGETABLE OR MUSTARD OIL, FOR SHALLOW FRYING
750 G/1½ LB AUBERGINES, CUT LENGTHWAYS INTO QUARTERS
125 G/4 OZ DRIED TAMARIND
2 LARGE ONIONS, SLICED
1 TEASPOON MUSTARD SEEDS
125 G/4 OZ GHEE OR BUTTER (SEE PAGE 11)
1½ TEASPOONS GROUND CORIANDER
1 FRESH GREEN CHILLI, DESEEDED AND CHOPPED
½ TEASPOON CHILLI POWDER
1 TABLESPOON DESICCATED COCONUT
3 GARLIC CLOVES, CHOPPED
1 TEASPOON GROUND TURMERIC
1 TEASPOON GARAM MASALA (SEE PAGE 11)
1 TEASPOON SUGAR
3 BAY LEAVES

Heat the oil in a heavy-based frying pan and sauté the aubergines until the skins just begin to turn crisp and brown. Remove and drain on kitchen paper. Soak the tamarind in boiling water to cover.

Fry the onions and mustard seeds in the ghee or butter in a large wok until golden brown, then add the coriander and the chilli and fry for 5 minutes more. Add the chilli powder, coconut, garlic, turmeric and garam masala and fry for a further 3 minutes.

Strain the tamarind liquid through a wire sieve set over a bowl, pressing to extract as much tamarind liquid as possible. Add the tamarind liquid to the wok, together with the sugar. Stir well and add the aubergines. Cover and cook for 10–15 minutes until the aubergines are tender, stirring occasionally but taking care to keep the aubergines whole.

Fry the bay leaves in a little hot oil for a few seconds and pour over the aubergines just before serving.

SERVES 4
PREPARATION TIME: 10 MINUTES
COOKING TIME: 30–40 MINUTES

Aubergines with Tomatoes

- 750 g/1½ lb aubergines, cut into 4 cm/1½ inch chunks
- juice of 1 lemon
- 175 g/6 oz ghee or butter (see page 11)
- 2 onions, thinly sliced
- 4 garlic cloves, thinly sliced
- 7.5 cm/3 inch piece fresh root ginger, peeled and thinly sliced
- 2 teaspoons black onion seeds (kalonji)
- 7.5 cm/3 inch piece cinnamon stick
- 2 teaspoons coriander seeds
- 2 teaspoons cumin seeds
- 2 teaspoons pepper
- 2 teaspoons salt
- 2 teaspoons garam masala (see page 11)
- 1½ teaspoons ground turmeric
- 1 teaspoon chilli powder
- 425 g/14 oz can chopped tomatoes
- 125 g/4 oz tomato purée
- dried red chillies, to garnish

Place the aubergine in a bowl and mix in the lemon juice.

Melt the ghee or butter in a large wok, add the onions, garlic and ginger and fry gently for 4–5 minutes, until soft. Add the black onion seeds, cinnamon, coriander and cumin and stir well. Fry for a further 2 minutes, then stir in the pepper, salt, garam masala, turmeric and chilli powder.

Add the tomatoes with their juice and the tomato purée, stir well and bring to the boil. Add 600 ml/1 pint boiling water, the aubergine pieces and lemon juice. Bring to the boil, lower the heat and simmer gently for 15–20 minutes, until soft. Garnish with dried red chillies and serve hot.

Serves 4–6

Preparation time: 15 minutes

Cooking time: 25–30 minutes

Dry Cauliflower and Potato Curry

50 G/2 OZ GHEE OR 4 TABLESPOONS VEGETABLE OIL (SEE PAGE 11)
2 TEASPOONS CUMIN SEEDS
1 ONION, DICED
2 POTATOES, CUT INTO CHUNKS
1 CAULIFLOWER, BROKEN INTO FLORETS
1 TEASPOON CHILLI POWDER
½ TEASPOON GROUND TURMERIC
2 TEASPOONS GROUND CORIANDER
2 TEASPOONS GARAM MASALA (SEE PAGE 11)
2 TEASPOONS MANGO POWDER OR JUICE OF 1 LEMON
SALT

Heat the ghee or oil in a wok, add the cumin seeds, then the onion and fry until lightly browned. Add the potatoes and fry for 2–3 minutes, then stir in the cauliflower pieces and continue frying for 5–6 minutes.

Stir in the chilli, turmeric, coriander, garam masala, mango powder or lemon juice and salt. Cover and cook gently for 10–15 minutes, until the potatoes and cauliflower are tender and the mixture is dry. If necessary add a little water during cooking to prevent the mixture sticking to the bottom of the wok, but avoid over-stirring, otherwise the cauliflower florets will disintegrate. Serve at once with chapatis.

SERVES 4
PREPARATION TIME: 15 MINUTES
COOKING TIME: 25–30 MINUTES

Potato, Pepper and Pea Curry

40 g/1½ oz ghee or 3 tablespoons vegetable oil (see page 11)
1½ teaspoons cumin seeds
1 small onion, chopped
500 g/1 lb potatoes, diced
1 teaspoon chilli powder
½ teaspoon ground turmeric
1½ teaspoons ground coriander
250 g/8 oz can chopped tomatoes
125 g/4 oz frozen peas
1 green pepper, deseeded and sliced
salt
chopped fresh coriander leaves, to garnish

Heat the ghee or oil in a large wok. Add the cumin seeds, then the onion and fry gently until lightly browned. Add the potatoes and fry for 3–4 minutes. Stir in the chilli powder, turmeric and coriander, and continue frying for 1–2 minutes.

Add the tomatoes, peas and peppers and stir well. Cover and cook gently for 1 minute, then stir in 200 ml/7 fl oz water and a little salt. Cook until the potatoes are tender. Serve hot, garnished with chopped coriander leaves.

Serves 4
Preparation time: 10 minutes
Cooking time: 15–20 minutes

Balti Courgettes

25 g/1 oz ghee or butter (see page 11)
1 small onion, chopped
a pinch of asafoetida (optional)
2 small potatoes, quartered
375 g/12 oz courgettes, sliced
½ teaspoon chilli powder
½ teaspoon ground turmeric
1 teaspoon ground coriander
½ teaspoon salt
½ teaspoon garam masala (see page 11)
chopped fresh coriander leaves, to garnish

Heat the ghee or butter in a large wok or heavy-based frying pan and fry the onion until it is tender. Add the asafoetida, if using, then add the potatoes and fry for about 2–3 minutes. Stir in the sliced courgettes, the chilli powder, turmeric, coriander and salt. Add 150 ml/¼ pint water, cover and cook gently for 8–10 minutes, until the potatoes are tender. Sprinkle on the garam masala and garnish with chopped coriander leaves. Serve immediately with chapatis.

Serves 4
Preparation time: 10 minutes
Cooking time: about 15 minutes

Balti Pumpkin

- 20 g/¾ oz dried tamarind, soaked in 150 ml/¼ pint hot water for 15 minutes
- 3 tablespoons vegetable oil
- ¼ teaspoon cumin seeds
- ¼ teaspoon mustard seeds
- ¼ teaspoon fenugreek seeds
- ¼ teaspoon black onion seeds (kalonji)
- ¼ teaspoon aniseeds
- 3 potatoes, cut into chunks
- 500 g/1 lb pumpkin, cubed
- 1 teaspoon chilli powder
- ½ teaspoon ground turmeric
- 1 teaspoon ground coriander
- 1 teaspoon sugar
- salt

Strain the tamarind liquid through a wire sieve set over a small bowl, pressing to extract as much pulp as possible. Repeat the process to extract any remaining pulp.

Heat the oil in a large wok and fry the cumin, mustard seeds, fenugreek, onion seeds and aniseeds for 30 seconds, then add the potatoes and fry for 2–3 minutes. Add the pumpkin, stir well and fry for 4–5 minutes.

Stir in the chilli, turmeric, coriander, sugar and salt and continue frying for 5–6 minutes. Add the tamarind pulp, cover and cook until the potatoes are tender, adding a little more water if necessary to prevent the mixture from sticking to the bottom of the wok. Serve hot.

Serves 4

Preparation time: 25 minutes

Cooking time: about 30 minutes

Balti Chickpeas

2 TABLESPOONS GHEE OR BUTTER (SEE PAGE 11)
1 ONION, CHOPPED
2.5 CM/1 INCH PIECE CINNAMON STICK
4 CLOVES
2 GARLIC CLOVES, CRUSHED
2.5 CM/1 INCH PIECE FRESH ROOT GINGER, PEELED AND CHOPPED
2 FRESH GREEN CHILLIES, FINELY CHOPPED
2 TEASPOONS GROUND CORIANDER
1 TEASPOON GROUND TURMERIC
150 G/5 OZ TOMATOES, CHOPPED
475 G/15 OZ CAN CHICKPEAS, DRAINED
1 TEASPOON GARAM MASALA (SEE PAGE 11)
1 TABLESPOON CHOPPED FRESH CORIANDER LEAVES

Heat the ghee or butter in a wok or heavy-based saucepan, add the onion and fry gently until golden. Add the cinnamon and cloves and fry for a few seconds, then add the garlic, ginger, chillies, ground coriander and turmeric and fry for 5 minutes. Add the tomatoes and fry until most of the liquid has evaporated.

Add the chickpeas and cook gently for 5–6 minutes or until heated through, adding a little water if necessary to prevent the mixture from sticking to the bottom of the wok. Add the garam masala and stir well. Sprinkle with the chopped coriander and serve at once.

SERVES 4
PREPARATION TIME: 20 MINUTES
COOKING TIME: 15–20 MINUTES

Chickpea and Potato Curry

4 SMALL POTATOES
4 TABLESPOONS VEGETABLE OIL
1 TEASPOON MUSTARD SEEDS
475 G/15 OZ CAN CHICKPEAS, DRAINED
1 TABLESPOON GROUND CORIANDER
1 TEASPOON CHILLI POWDER
250 G/8 OZ CAN TOMATOES, CHOPPED WITH THE JUICE
1 TABLESPOON TOMATO PURÉE
1 TABLESPOON BROWN SUGAR
SALT
SPRIGS OF FRESH CORIANDER LEAVES, TO GARNISH

Cook the potatoes in boiling salted water until they are tender. Drain and cool, then cut into cubes.

Heat the oil in a wok or heavy-based frying pan, add the mustard seeds and fry until they begin to pop. Add the chickpeas and potatoes and toss them in the oil and seeds. Stir in the ground coriander and chilli powder.

Add the tomatoes, tomato purée, sugar and salt, stir well then cover and heat through. Garnish with sprigs of fresh coriander and serve with naan.

SERVES 4
PREPARATION TIME: 30 MINUTES, PLUS COOLING
COOKING TIME: 15–20 MINUTES

Balti Beans

125 G/4 OZ GHEE OR BUTTER (SEE PAGE 11)
2 ONIONS, FINELY CHOPPED
3 GARLIC CLOVES, CRUSHED
2.5 CM/1 INCH PIECE FRESH ROOT GINGER, PEELED AND GRATED
1 TABLESPOON GROUND CORIANDER
1 TEASPOON GARAM MASALA (SEE PAGE 11)
1 TEASPOON CHILLI POWDER
1 TEASPOON GROUND TURMERIC
425 G/14 OZ CAN CHOPPED TOMATOES
1 TEASPOON SUGAR
475 G/15 OZ CAN BUTTER BEANS, DRAINED
475 G/15 OZ CAN KIDNEY BEANS, DRAINED
475 G/15 OZ CAN HARICOT BEANS OR CANNELLINI BEANS, DRAINED
SALT
5–6 SPRIGS OF FRESH CORIANDER LEAVES, CHOPPED, TO GARNISH

Heat the ghee or butter in a wok or heavy-based frying pan, add the onions and fry for 5–10 minutes, until they are lightly browned.

Add the garlic and ginger and fry for a few seconds only, then add the coriander, garam masala, chilli powder and turmeric and stir-fry for a few seconds.

Stir in the tomatoes, sugar and salt to taste. Lower the heat and simmer for 10 minutes. Add the drained beans, stir thoroughly, then cover and heat through gently.

Garnish the beans with the chopped coriander and serve at once with chapatis.

Serves 6–8
Preparation time: 25 minutes
Cooking time: 30–35 minutes

Kidney Bean Curry

125 g/4 oz vegetable oil
2 teaspoons cumin seeds
1 large onion, chopped
425 g/14 oz can chopped tomatoes
1 tablespoon ground coriander
1 teaspoon chilli powder
1 teaspoon sugar
1 teaspoon salt
2 x 475 g/15 oz cans kidney beans, drained

Heat the oil in a wok or frying pan, add the cumin seeds and chopped onion and fry until the onion is lightly browned.

Stir in the tomatoes and fry for a few seconds, then add the coriander, chilli, sugar and salt and stir well. Lower the heat and cook for about 5–7 minutes.

Add the drained kidney beans, stir carefully but thoroughly and heat for 10–15 minutes. Serve at once with chapatis.

Serves 4–6
Preparation time: 15 minutes
Cooking time: 30–35 minutes

Lentil Curry

250 g/8 oz red lentils (masoor dal), washed and drained
125 g/4 oz ghee or butter (see page 11)
1 large onion, finely chopped
2 garlic cloves, crushed
50 g/2 oz piece fresh root ginger, peeled and chopped
2 tablespoons ground coriander
1 teaspoon garam masala (see page 11)
1 teaspoon chilli powder
1 teaspoon ground cardamom
425 g/14 oz can chopped tomatoes
5 tablespoons tomato purée
2 teaspoons sugar
salt
fresh coriander leaves, to garnish

Place the lentils and 450 ml/3/4 pint water in a pan and cook, uncovered, over a gentle heat for about 20–25 minutes, or until the lentils are tender.

Meanwhile, heat the ghee or butter in a wok over a medium heat, add the onion and fry for 4–5 minutes, until golden. Add the garlic and ginger and fry for a few seconds. Add the spices and stir-fry for 2 minutes. Stir in the tomatoes and tomato purée and fry for a further 2 minutes. Add the sugar, 150 ml/1/4 pint water, salt to taste and stir well. Partly cover, and cook over a gentle heat for about 15 minutes, or until most of the liquid has evaporated. Stir the sauce into the lentils and simmer for a further 5–10 minutes. Garnish with fresh coriander and serve at once.

Serves 4
Preparation time: 10 minutes
Cooking time: 25–30 minutes

Hyderabadi Dal

175 G/6 OZ RED LENTILS (MASOOR DAL) WASHED AND DRAINED
6 GARLIC CLOVES
2.5 CM/1 INCH PIECE FRESH ROOT GINGER, GRATED
1 TEASPOON GROUND TURMERIC
3 FRESH GREEN CHILLIES
12 CURRY LEAVES
175 G/6 OZ DRIED TAMARIND, SOAKED IN 300 ML/½ PINT HOT WATER FOR 30 MINUTES
1 TABLESPOON TOMATO PURÉE
2 TEASPOONS SALT
2 TEASPOONS VEGETABLE OIL
1 TEASPOON CUMIN SEEDS
4 DRIED RED CHILLIES

Place the lentils in a large saucepan with 900 ml/1½ pints water, 2 crushed garlic cloves, the ginger, turmeric, the green chillies and 6 curry leaves. Bring to the boil, then lower the heat and simmer until the lentils have broken up. Add a little extra water if the mixture begins to get dry.

Strain the tamarind through a wire sieve set over a small bowl, pressing to extract as much liquid as possible. Add to the lentil mixture with the tomato purée and a little salt and simmer for a further 15 minutes. Mash the cooked lentils with a potato masher or blend briefly in a liquidizer (first remove the whole chillies and curry leaves) until smooth and creamy.

In a wok, heat the oil until very hot, then add the remaining garlic cloves, halved, the remaining curry leaves, the cumin seeds and dried red chillies. As soon as the garlic is golden, pour the oil and spices over the lentils and cover. Leave for 1 minute, then serve.

SERVES 4
PREPARATION TIME: 20 MINUTES
COOKING TIME: ABOUT 35 MINUTES

Spinach and Moong Dal

- 75 G/3 OZ PLAIN FLOUR OR CHICKPEA FLOUR (GRAM FLOUR OR BESAN)
- ½ TEASPOON GROUND TURMERIC
- 250 ML/8 OZ NATURAL YOGURT
- 12 TABLESPOONS SPLIT YELLOW LENTILS (MOONG DAL), WASHED AND DRAINED
- 750 G/1½ LB FRESH SPINACH, WASHED, SHAKEN DRY AND ROUGHLY CHOPPED
- 2½ TEASPOONS SALT
- 2 TABLESPOONS LEMON JUICE
- ½ TEASPOON CAYENNE PEPPER
- FRESHLY GROUND BLACK PEPPER
- 2 TABLESPOONS VEGETABLE OIL
- 1 TEASPOON ASAFOETIDA (OPTIONAL)
- 1 TEASPOON CUMIN SEEDS
- 2 DRIED RED CHILLIES, DESEEDED AND CRUSHED

Sift the flour and turmeric into a small bowl. Gradually stir in 4 tablespoons of water to give a smooth paste. In another bowl, whisk the yogurt until smooth, then gradually stir in 1.3 litres/2¼ pints water. Beat the flour mixture together with the yogurt mixture. Pour into a large saucepan and bring to the boil over a gentle heat.

Add the lentils, spinach, salt, lemon juice and cayenne. Bring back to the boil, lower the heat and simmer for 1½ hours, stirring every 10 minutes. Add a little hot water if it becomes too thick.

Taste and adjust the seasoning, then cover and keep warm.

Heat the oil in a wok. Add the asafoetida, if using, followed immediately by the cumin seeds and chillies. As soon as the chillies darken, stir the mixture once and pour the sizzling hot spices over the lentils. Cover and leave for 1 minute, then serve at once.

SERVES 4

PREPARATION TIME: 20 MINUTES

COOKING TIME: 2 HOURS

Sesame Butter Beans

4 TABLESPOONS VEGETABLE OIL
1 TEASPOON CUMIN SEEDS
1 LARGE ONION, CHOPPED
125 G/4 OZ SESAME SEEDS, FINELY GROUND
1 TABLESPOON GROUND CORIANDER
425 G/14 OZ CAN CHOPPED TOMATOES
2 TEASPOONS SALT
2 TEASPOONS SUGAR
1 TEASPOON CHILLI POWDER
1 TEASPOON GROUND TURMERIC
2 x 475 G/15 OZ CANS BUTTER BEANS, DRAINED
CHOPPED FRESH CORIANDER, TO GARNISH

Heat the oil in a wok or heavy-based saucepan, add the cumin seeds and fry until they begin to crackle. Add the onion and fry until soft. Add the ground sesame seeds and fry for 3–5 minutes, then add the ground coriander and fry for a further minute. Stir in the tomatoes, salt, sugar, chilli powder and turmeric. Mix well and cook the sauce for 3–5 minutes. Add the drained beans and stir carefully until well coated with the sauce. Simmer until the beans are thoroughly hot. Sprinkle with chopped coriander and serve.

SERVES 4
PREPARARTION TIME: 20 MINUTES
COOKING TIME: 25–30 MINUTES

SIDE DISHES

AND CHUTNEYS

WHILE THE 'ORIGINAL' BALTIS WERE ONE-DISH MEALS, QUICK TO COOK AND EAT – AND SERVED WITH BREAD – COMPLETE IN THEMSELVES, THE ACCOMPANIMENT OF TANGY OR FRUITY CHUTNEYS OR COOL YOGURT RAITAS MAKES ANY BALTI INTO A FEAST. THEY CAN ALSO BE SERVED WITH CRISP POPPADUMS AS INFORMAL FIRST COURSES OR DIPS – NO NEED TO CLEAR THEM AWAY WHEN THE BALTI PAN COMES TO THE TABLE.

Cucumber Raita

250 ML/8 FL OZ NATURAL YOGURT
½ CUCUMBER, GRATED OR SLICED
1 TEASPOON PEPPER
1–2 SPRIGS OF FRESH CORIANDER LEAVES, CHOPPED
1 FRESH GREEN OR RED CHILLI, DESEEDED AND VERY FINELY CHOPPED (OPTIONAL)
SALT

Beat the yogurt in a bowl. Stir in the other ingredients, adding salt and chilli to taste and reserving a little chopped chilli to garnish. Mix well and chill in the refrigerator.

Garnish the raita with the reserved chilli.

SERVES 4–6

PREPARATION TIME: 5–7 MINUTES, PLUS CHILLING

Aubergine Raita

- VEGETABLE OIL FOR DEEP-FRYING
- 375 G/12 OZ AUBERGINE, SLICED INTO 3 MM/⅛ INCH ROUNDS
- 300 ML/½ PINT NATURAL YOGURT
- 2 TEASPOONS CUMIN SEEDS, DRY-ROASTED AND COARSELY GROUND
- 1–2 TEASPOONS CHILLI POWDER
- SALT

Heat the oil in a large wok or heavy-based frying pan and fry the aubergine slices until they are golden brown. Remove and drain well on kitchen paper.

Season the yogurt with a little salt, then pour into a shallow serving dish. Add the fried aubergine and sprinkle with ground cumin and chilli powder. Serve immediately.

Serves 4–6

Preparation time: 10 minutes

Cooking time: 15 minutes

Mixed Vegetable Raita

300 ml/½ pint natural yogurt
1–2 teaspoons pepper or chilli powder
¼ cucumber, diced
1 small onion, diced
1–2 potatoes, boiled and cubed
2–3 tomatoes, chopped
125 g/4 oz radishes, trimmed and sliced
1–2 celery sticks, diced
1 fresh green chilli, deseeded and very finely chopped (optional)
salt

To garnish:
1–2 sprigs of fresh coriander leaves, chopped
a slice of radish

In a large bowl, beat the yogurt to a smooth consistency with the pepper or chilli powder, adding salt to taste. Add the vegetables and mix well. Sprinkle on the green chilli and then chill in the refrigerator before serving.
Garnish with coriander leaves and a slice of radish.

Serves 4–6

Preparation time: 8–10 minutes, plus chilling

Mint Chutney

- 2 tablespoons desiccated coconut, lightly toasted
- 2–3 fresh green chillies, deseeded and chopped
- 1 large bunch of fresh mint, leaves only, chopped
- 3 tablespoons lemon juice
- 1 teaspoon sugar
- 1½ teaspoons salt
- A pinch of freshly ground black pepper

Grind the toasted coconut in an electric grinder, then add all the other ingredients and blend to a creamy consistency. Alternatively, pound the coconut in a mortar, with a pestle, gradually pounding in the remaining ingredients. Serve lightly chilled.

Serves 4–6

Preparation time: 10 minutes, plus chilling

Coriander Chutney

25 G/1 OZ DESICCATED COCONUT
150 ML/¼ PINT NATURAL YOGURT
125 G/4 OZ FRESH CORIANDER LEAVES AND SOME FINE STALKS
JUICE OF 1 LEMON
2 FRESH GREEN CHILLIES, DESEEDED AND CHOPPED
1 TEASPOON SUGAR
1 TEASPOON SALT

Mix the coconut with the yogurt and leave to marinate in the refrigerator for 1 hour.

Place in a food processor or liquidizer with the remaining ingredients and blend until smooth. Chill the chutney before serving.

SERVES 4

PREPARATION TIME: 10 MINUTES, PLUS 1 HOUR MARINATING AND CHILLING

Green Chutney

- 50 g/2 oz dried tamarind, soaked in 300 ml/½ pint hot water for 15 minutes, or 125 g/4 oz green unripe mango flesh
- 175 g/6 oz fresh or desiccated coconut
- 4–6 large or 8–10 small sprigs of coriander leaves, stalks discarded
- 1–2 fresh green chillies, deseeded and roughly chopped
- 25 g/1 oz fresh root ginger, peeled
- 1 teaspoon cumin seeds
- ½–1 teaspoon salt
- 1 small onion, finely chopped

Strain the tamarind liquid through a wire sieve set over a small bowl, pressing to extract as much pulp as possible. Repeat this process to extract any remaining pulp.

Grind the coconut, coriander leaves, chilli, ginger, cumin seeds and tamarind pulp to a smooth paste. If using the mango add a little water. Add salt to taste and stir in the chopped onion. Serve the chutney lightly chilled.

Serves 6–8

Preparation time: about 30 minutes, plus chilling

Tomato Chutney

1 ONION, FINELY CHOPPED
3 TEASPOONS CHOPPED FRESH CORIANDER
½ TEASPOON CHOPPED FRESH MINT
2 FRESH RED OR GREEN CHILLIES, DESEEDED AND FINELY CHOPPED
3 TABLESPOONS LEMON JUICE
1½ TEASPOONS SALT
A PINCH OF PEPPER
4 TOMATOES (FIRM ONES WHICH ARE NOT QUITE RIPE)
A SPRIG OF MINT, TO GARNISH

Mix all the ingredients together, except the tomatoes, and put them in the refrigerator to chill.

Finely chop the tomatoes and add them to the mixture just before serving. (If the tomatoes are added too soon they will make the chutney watery.) Serve garnished with mint.

SERVES 4

PREPARATION TIME: 15 MINUTES, PLUS CHILLING

Sesame Chutney

125 G/4 OZ DRIED TAMARIND
4 TABLESPOONS SESAME SEEDS
2 TEASPOONS SALT
2 TABLESPOONS CHOPPED FRESH CORIANDER
3 GREEN CHILLIES
A GENEROUS PINCH OF BLACK PEPPER

Place the tamarind and 75 ml/3 fl oz water in a small pan and bring to the boil. Cover and simmer for 10 minutes. Remove from the heat and leave to stand for 1 hour. Mash well, then strain the tamarind through a wire sieve set over a bowl, pressing well to extract as much pulp as possible.

Roast the sesame seeds until lightly browned, then cool and grind them finely in a coffee grinder or spice mill. Place the sesame seeds with all the remaining ingredients in a liquidizer and blend them together to make a smooth paste. Serve in a small bowl.

SERVES 4

PREPARATION TIME: 25 MINUTES, PLUS 1 HOUR SOAKING

Gooseberry Chutney

- 250 g/8 oz unripe gooseberries
- ½ onion, finely chopped
- 1 small green pepper, deseeded and finely chopped
- 1 fresh green chilli, finely chopped
- 2 tablespoons chopped fresh coriander
- 1 teaspoon honey
- ½ teaspoon pepper
- 2 teaspoons salt

Top, tail and quarter the gooseberries, then mix them with all the other ingredients and serve chilled.

Serves 6

Preparation time: 15 minutes, plus chilling

Mango Chutney

6 green mangoes
about 2 teaspoons salt
3–4 fresh red chillies, roughly chopped, or 2 teaspoons chilli powder
300 ml/½ pint malt vinegar
400 g/13 oz sugar
25–40 g/1–1½ oz fresh root ginger, peeled and chopped
125 g/4 oz mixed unsalted nuts and raisins, roughly chopped (optional)

Peel the mangoes and grate the flesh into a large bowl. Sprinkle with 2 teaspoons of the salt and set aside for 30 minutes.

Either grind the chillies or mix the chilli powder with a little of the vinegar to a fine paste. Place the remaining vinegar in a pan, add the sugar and simmer gently, stirring, until the sugar dissolves. Squeeze the grated mangoes with the back of a spoon to extract the juice, and discard the juice. Add the mango flesh to the pan and simmer gently for a further 5–6 minutes. Add the ginger and the chilli paste and mix well. Cook for 10–12 minutes.

Taste and add salt, if necessary. Stir in the chopped nuts and raisins and cook for 4 minutes. Remove from the heat and leave to cool. Bottle in airtight jars with vinegar-proof tops.

Serves 6
Preparation time: 25 minutes, plus 30 minutes salting
Cooking time: about 30 minutes

Mixed Vegetable Chutney

- 25 g/1 oz dried tamarind, soaked in 150 ml/¼ pint hot water for 15 minutes
- 2 tablespoons vegetable oil
- 1 teaspoon mustard seeds
- 1 small onion, diced
- 1 sweet potato, peeled and diced (optional)
- 1 carrot, diced
- 50 g/2 oz sweetcorn kernels
- 1 kg/2 lb tomatoes, skinned and chopped
- 1 teaspoon salt
- 1 teaspoon chilli powder
- ½ teaspoon ground turmeric
- 50 g/2 oz fresh root ginger, peeled and grated
- 3 tablespoons soft brown sugar
- 200 ml/7 fl oz malt vinegar
- 125 g/4 oz sultanas and raisins
- ½ cucumber, chopped and juice discarded

Strain the tamarind liquid through a wire sieve set over a small bowl, pressing to extract as much pulp as possible. Repeat this process to extract any remaining pulp.

Heat the oil in a pan and fry the mustard seeds. When they begin to pop, add the onion, sweet potato, carrot and sweetcorn, and fry for 4–5 minutes. Add the tomatoes, salt and chilli powder, then cover and simmer until the tomatoes are soft.

Stir in the turmeric, grated ginger, sugar, vinegar, tamarind pulp, sultanas and raisins. Gently simmer until the sugar syrup is thick and the vegetables are tender, adding a little water if necessary. Add the cucumber and simmer for 1 minute. Leave to cool, then cover tightly and chill in the refrigerator. This chutney should be eaten within 7 days.

Serves 6

Preparation time: 35–40 minutes

Cooking time: about 35 minutes

Spiced Fruit and Vegetables

- 1 onion, chopped
- 4 celery sticks, chopped
- 1 tablespoon vegetable oil
- 1 tablespoon curry powder
- 1 tablespoon flour
- 300 ml/½ pint light stock or water
- 2.5 cm/1 inch piece fresh root ginger, finely chopped, or 1 teaspoon ground ginger
- juice and grated rind of 1 lemon
- 425 g/14 oz can apricot halves, drained
- 2 bananas, thickly sliced
- 500 g/1 lb cooking apples, peeled, cored and quartered
- 125 g/4 oz raisins
- 150 ml/¼ pint soured cream

Fry the onion and celery in the oil until golden brown. Stir in the curry powder and flour and cook gently for 2–3 minutes, stirring constantly. Mix the stock or water with the ginger and gradually stir into the pan. Add the lemon juice and rind, apricots, bananas, apples and raisins. Stir well and cook, covered, over low heat until the fruit is tender. Just before serving, stir in the soured cream.

Serves 6

Preparation time: 20 minutes

Cooking time: 20–25 minutes

Aubergine Bhartha

- 4–5 AUBERGINES
- 6 TABLESPOONS VEGETABLE OIL
- 1 FRESH GREEN CHILLI, DESEEDED
- 10 PEPPERCORNS
- 2 GARLIC CLOVES
- ½ TEASPOON GROUND TURMERIC
- 3 ONIONS, CHOPPED
- A SMALL PIECE OF FRESH ROOT GINGER, PEELED AND CHOPPED
- 4 TOMATOES, SKINNED AND MASHED
- ¼ TEASPOON CHILLI POWDER
- SALT AND PEPPER
- CHOPPED FRESH CORIANDER LEAVES, TO GARNISH

Baste the aubergines with a little oil and bake in a preheated oven, 180°C (350°F), Gas Mark 4, for about 45 minutes, or until tender. When cool, remove the skins and mash the pulp.

Using an electric grinder, spice mill or pestle and mortar, grind the chilli, peppercorns, garlic and turmeric together to form a paste. Heat 5 tablespoons of oil in a large wok and stir-fry the onions until golden brown. Add the spice paste to the onions with the ginger and stir-fry for 2 minutes.

Add the mashed aubergines and stir-fry until lightly browned. Add the tomatoes, chilli powder and salt and pepper to taste. Cover and cook for 15 minutes over a low heat. Chill in the refrigerator before serving, garnished with coriander leaves.

SERVES 8

PREPARATION TIME: 40 MINUTES, PLUS CHILLING

COOKING TIME: 1 HOUR 10 MINUTES

Onion Salad

1 LARGE ONION, VERY THINLY SLICED
JUICE OF 1 LEMON
1 GREEN CHILLI, VERY FINELY CHOPPED
½ TEASPOON SALT
½ TEASPOON CASTER SUGAR
A FEW SPRIGS OF CORIANDER OR MINT, TO GARNISH

Soak the onion in a bowl of iced water for 30 minutes. Drain, pat dry with kitchen paper and separate into rings. Mix the lemon juice, chilli, salt and sugar until the sugar dissolves, then sprinkle over the onion. Cover and chill in the refrigerator before serving.

SERVES 4

PREPARATION TIME: 10 MINUTES, PLUS 30 MINUTES SOAKING

BREADS

ALTHOUGH BALTI IS A NEW, STILL EVOLVING CUISINE, ONE TRADITION IS FIRMLY ESTABLISHED: BREAD, NOT RICE, IS THE INDISPENSABLE ACCOMPANIMENT TO ANY MEAL. THERE IS A HUGE VARIETY OF BREADS FROM NORTHERN INDIA AND PAKISTAN: SOME ARE QUITE FLAT, COOKED IN A CAST-IRON PAN ON TOP OF THE COOKER OR ON THE SIDE OF A CLAY OVEN, OTHERS ARE DEEP-FRIED AND PUFF UP INTO CUSHION SHAPES.

Chapati

250 G/8 OZ PLAIN WHOLEMEAL FLOUR
1 TEASPOON SALT
ABOUT 200 ML/7 FL OZ WATER
GHEE OR BUTTER FOR COOKING
(SEE PAGE 11)

Sift the flour and salt into a bowl. Make a well in the centre and gradually stir in just enough water to form a soft, supple dough. Knead for 10 minutes, then cover with a damp tea towel and leave in a cool place for 30 minutes.

Knead again very thoroughly, then divide into 12 pieces. Roll out each piece on a lightly floured surface into a thin round.

Lightly grease a griddle or heavy-based frying pan with a little ghee or butter and place over a moderate heat. Add a chapati and cook until blisters appear. Press down with a fish slice, then turn and cook the other side until lightly coloured. Remove from the pan and keep warm, wrapped in a tea towel, while cooking the rest.

Brush a little ghee or butter on one side and serve warm.

MAKES 12

PREPARATION TIME: 30 MINUTES, PLUS 30 MINUTES RESTING

COOKING TIME: ABOUT 45 MINUTES

Chapati with Onion

250 G/8 OZ PLAIN OR WHOLEMEAL FLOUR
1½ TEASPOONS SALT
4 TEASPOONS GHEE OR UNSALTED BUTTER, MELTED (SEE PAGE 11)
ABOUT 200 ML/7 FL OZ WATER
2 ONIONS, VERY FINELY CHOPPED
2 FRESH GREEN CHILLIES, VERY FINELY CHOPPED

Sift the flour and 1 teaspoon of the salt into a large mixing bowl. Make a well in the centre and add 2 teaspoons of the melted ghee or butter, together with enough water to make a supple dough. Knead for 10 minutes, then cover with a damp tea towel and leave in a cool place for 30 minutes.

Mix the onions and chillies with the remaining ½ teaspoon of salt. Place in a sieve and squeeze out any liquid.

Knead the dough again, then divide into 12 pieces. Roll out each piece on a lightly floured surface into a thin round. Put a little of the onion and chilli mixture in the centre, fold the dough over and form into a ball, then roll out carefully into a round.

Cook as for Chapati (see recipe on page 140), using the remaining ghee or butter to grease the pan.

MAKES 12

PREPARATION TIME: 30 MINUTES, PLUS 30 MINUTES RESTING

COOKING TIME: 45 MINUTES

Paratha

250 G/8 OZ PLAIN WHOLEMEAL FLOUR
1 TEASPOON SALT
ABOUT 200 ML/7 FL OZ WATER
50–75 G/2–3 OZ GHEE OR BUTTER, MELTED (SEE PAGE 11)

Make the dough as for Chapati (see recipe on page 140) and leave for 30 minutes. Knead again, then divide into 6 pieces. Roll out each piece on a lightly floured surface into a thin round. Brush with melted ghee or butter and fold in half; brush the top with some ghee and fold in half again. Carefully roll out again to form a circle about 3 mm/1/8 inch thick.

Lightly grease a griddle or heavy-based frying pan with a little ghee or butter and place over a moderate heat. Add a paratha and cook for 1 minute. Lightly brush the top with a little melted ghee or butter and turn over. Brush all round the edge with ghee or butter and cook until golden. Remove from the pan and keep warm while cooking the rest. Serve warm.

MAKES 6
PREPARATION TIME: 30 MINUTES, PLUS 30 MINUTES RESTING
COOKING TIME: 15 MINUTES

Kachori

250 g/8 oz plain wholemeal flour
½ teaspoon salt
125–175 ml/4–6 fl oz water
Filling:
50 g/2 oz lentils, washed and soaked for 3 hours
½ teaspoon cumin seeds
½ teaspoon aniseeds
1–2 tablespoons vegetable oil
a pinch of asafoetida (optional)
1 small fresh green chilli, deseeded and very finely chopped, or ½ teaspoon chilli powder
a pinch of salt
vegetable oil for deep-frying

Sift the flour and salt and make a well in the centre. Gradually add just enough water to make a dough. Knead well for 5–10 minutes, cover with a damp tea towel and set aside.

To make the filling, drain the lentils and grind to a thick, coarse paste with a little water. Dry-roast the cumin seeds and aniseeds for 30 seconds and grind coarsely. Heat 1 tablespoon of oil in a wok and sprinkle in the asafoetida and lentil paste. Add the chilli, salt, the ground cumin and aniseed. Fry for 5 minutes, adding a little more oil if necessary. Leave to cool.

Divide the dough into 12–14 pieces. Roll each piece into a ball and make a depression in the middle. Press about 1 teaspoon of filling in the depression and shape the dough into a ball, enclosing the filling. Carefully roll out into a 7 cm / 3 inch round.

Heat 5–6 cm/2–2½ inches of oil in a large frying pan and fry the kachoris a few at a time until golden brown on both sides. Remove with a slotted spoon and drain on kitchen paper. Keep warm while frying the remaining kachoris. Serve hot with chutney.

Makes 12–14
Preparation time: 30 minutes, plus 3 hours soaking
Cooking time: about 30 minutes

Puri

250 g/8 oz plain wholemeal flour
½ teaspoon salt
about 125–175 ml/4–6 fl oz water
vegetable oil for deep-frying

Sift the flour and salt into a bowl and make a well in the centre. Gradually add just enough water to make a dough. Knead well for 5–10 minutes, cover with a damp tea towel and set aside for about 30 minutes.

Divide the dough into 12–14 pieces. On a lightly floured surface roll out each portion into a flat 7 cm/3 inch round.

Heat the oil to 180–190°C (350–375°F), or until a cube of bread browns in 30 seconds. Slide in one puri at a time and fry on both sides until golden brown. It will quickly swell up in the oil.

Lift out the puri with a slotted spoon and drain on kitchen paper. Continue frying the puris and stack in layers, alternating the thin and thick sides to prevent sticking. Keep wrapped in a clean tea towel or place in a covered container while you fry the remaining puris. Serve warm.

Makes 12–14
Preparation time: 20 minutes, plus 30 minutes resting
Cooking time: about 30 minutes

Naan

15 G/½ OZ FRESH YEAST
¼ TEASPOON SUGAR
500 G/1 LB SELF-RAISING FLOUR
1 TEASPOON SALT
150 ML/¼ PINT TEPID MILK
150 ML/¼ PINT NATURAL YOGURT (AT ROOM TEMPERATURE)
2 TABLESPOONS MELTED GHEE, BUTTER OR VEGETABLE OIL (SEE PAGE 11)

TO DECORATE:
2–3 TABLESPOONS MELTED GHEE OR BUTTER (SEE PAGE 11)
1 TABLESPOON POPPY SEEDS OR SESAME SEEDS

Put the yeast in a small bowl with the sugar and about 2 tablespoons warm water. Mix well until the yeast has dissolved, then leave in a warm place for 15 minutes or until the mixture is frothy.

Sift the flour and salt into a large bowl. Make a well in the centre and pour in the yeast mixture, milk, yogurt and butter or oil. Mix well to a smooth dough and turn on to a lightly floured surface. Knead well for about 10 minutes, until smooth and elastic. Place in the bowl, cover with cling film or a damp tea towel and leave to rise in a warm place for 1–1½ hours, or until doubled in size.

Turn on to a lightly floured surface, knead for a few minutes, then divide into 6 pieces. Pat or roll each piece into a round.

Arrange on warmed baking sheets and place in a preheated oven, 240°C (475°F), Gas Mark 9, for 10 minutes. Brush with ghee or butter and sprinkle with the poppy or sesame seeds. Serve warm.

MAKES 6
PREPARATION TIME: 30 MINUTES, PLUS 1¼–1¾ HOURS RISING
COOKING TIME: 10 MINUTES

DESSERTS

AND DRINKS

A COOL YOGURT DRINK IS VERY REFRESHING WITH SPICY FOOD, AND A VERY COLD OR VERY SWEET PUDDING IS NOT ONLY TRADITIONAL, IT IS ALSO A SURPRISINGLY GOOD WAY TO ROUND OFF A BALTI DINNER. SERVE THESE DESSERTS AND SWEETMEATS IN SMALL QUANTITIES: THEY ARE NOT MEANT TO FILL YOU UP, BUT TO PROVIDE A CONTRASTING END TO THE MEAL.

Kulfi

250 G/8 OZ BLANCHED ALMONDS
1.8 LITRES/3 PINTS MILK
250 G/8 OZ CASTER SUGAR
300 ML/½ PINT DOUBLE CREAM
2 TABLESPOONS ROSE WATER

Place the almonds in a bowl, cover with cold water and set aside. Reserve 300 ml/½ pint of the milk and bring the rest to the boil in a large heavy-based or nonstick saucepan. Simmer until the milk is reduced by half, stirring from time to time to ensure that any skin or solids that cling to the side of the pan are well mixed in.

Drain the almonds and place three-quarters of them in a liquidizer with the reserved milk. Blend the mixture for a few seconds until the almonds are roughly ground; the mixture should be crunchy. Add the almond mixture and sugar to the hot milk and continue simmering for a further 10–20 minutes, stirring constantly. Remove the pan from the heat and leave to cool to room temperature, then place in the refrigerator until well chilled.

Roughly chop the remaining almonds and add them to the chilled milk with the double cream and rose water, stirring thoroughly so that the ingredients are well mixed. Pour into moulds – cone-shaped metal ones are traditional – and freeze until solid. Transfer to the refrigerator 20 minutes before serving, then turn out and serve.

SERVES 8
PREPARATION TIME: 1 HOUR, PLUS FREEZING
COOKING TIME: ABOUT 40 MINUTES

Mango Kulfi

397 G/13 OZ CAN CONDENSED MILK
300 ML/½ PINT DOUBLE CREAM
125 G/4 OZ GRANULATED SUGAR
1 TABLESPOON FINELY CHOPPED ALMONDS
1 TABLESPOON FINELY CHOPPED PISTACHIOS
400 G/13 OZ CAN MANGO SLICES OR PULP
1 TABLESPOON KEWRA WATER OR LEMON JUICE

Boil the milk and cream together with the sugar, stirring constantly until the sugar dissolves, then leave to simmer on a very low heat for about 30 minutes.

Stir in the almonds and pistachios, and cool to room temperature by standing the saucepan in a bowl of cold water.

If using mango slices, drain off half the juice from the can and crush the slices with the remaining juice. Add the mango to the milk mixture, then add the kewra water or lemon juice and beat well. Pour into moulds and freeze until the kulfi is solid. Turn out and serve.

SERVES 4
PREPARATION TIME: 15 MINUTES, PLUS FREEZING
COOKING TIME: 40 MINUTES

Pistachio Kulfi

125 G/4 OZ UNSALTED PISTACHIO NUTS, SHELLED, PLUS EXTRA TO DECORATE
397 G/13 OZ CAN CONDENSED MILK
300 ML/½ PINT DOUBLE CREAM
125 G/4 OZ CASTER SUGAR
2 EGGS, SEPARATED
2 DROPS ALMOND ESSENCE
2 DROPS GREEN FOOD COLOURING

Place the pistachios in a basin, cover with cold water and set aside.

Heat the condensed milk in a saucepan and add the double cream and the sugar, stirring until the sugar dissolves. Beat the egg yolks into the milk together with the almond essence and the green colouring, then leave the mixture to simmer gently.

Drain the pistachios and rub off the skins. Chop the nuts finely and add to the saucepan, beating in well. Bring to the boil, then leave to cool to room temperature. Place in the refrigerator until the mixture is nearly set.

Whisk the egg whites until they form peaks. Fold the beaten egg whites into the chilled mixture until evenly mixed, then pour into moulds and freeze until firm. Turn out and serve decorated with chopped pistachio nuts.

SERVES 4

PREPARATION TIME: 40 MINUTES, PLUS FREEZING

COOKING TIME: 15 MINUTES

Jallebi

- 375 g/12 oz plain flour
- 150 ml/¼ pint natural yogurt
- 25 g/1 oz dried yeast
- 500 g/1 lb sugar
- a pinch of saffron
- 6 cardamom seeds
- 6 cloves
- vegetable oil for deep-frying
- icing sugar, to decorate

Sift the flour into a bowl and add the yogurt, yeast and enough cold water to form a batter the consistency of double cream. Cover and leave in a warm place for about 4 hours to ferment.

Prepare the syrup by dissolving the sugar in 600 ml/1 pint water in a saucepan, together with the saffron, cardamoms and cloves. Bring to the boil and evaporate until a heavy syrup is obtained.

Heat the oil in a large wok to 180–190°C (350–375°F), or until a cube of bread browns in 30 seconds. Using an icing bag or a narrow funnel, swirl the batter into the hot oil to form the traditional whirls. Cook for about 1 minute, turning constantly, until the jallebi is a light brown colour.

Remove with a slotted spoon, drain on kitchen paper, then immerse in the syrup for approximately 5 minutes, so that the syrup runs through the pipes of the jallebi without making the crisp outside become soggy.

Remove the jallebi from the syrup; drain and dust with icing sugar. Serve warm.

Serves 4

Preparation time: 20 minutes, plus 4 hours fermenting

Cooking time: 20 minutes

Phirni

25 G/1 OZ RICE
600 ML/1 PINT MILK
125 G/4 OZ SUGAR
5 DROPS KEWRA WATER
25 G/1 OZ MIXED PISTACHIOS AND ALMONDS, CHOPPED, PLUS EXTRA, SPLIT IN HALF, TO DECORATE

Soak the rice in 150 ml/¼ pint water for 1½ hours, then drain and grind in a liquidizer to form a smooth paste.

Heat the milk slowly in a saucepan and stir in the rice paste. Stir until the mixture begins to thicken. Remove from the heat and add the sugar.

When the sugar is fully dissolved, bring to the boil and simmer for 2 minutes. Leave to cool, then add the kewra water and the chopped almonds and pistachios.

Serve chilled, decorated with split almonds and pistachios.

SERVES 4
PREPARATION TIME: 10 MINUTES, PLUS 1½ HOURS SOAKING, PLUS CHILLING
COOKING TIME: 10–15 MINUTES

Almond Barfi

750 ML/1¼ PINTS MILK
50 G/2 OZ CASTER SUGAR
50 G/2 OZ GROUND ALMONDS
SEEDS FROM 4–6 CARDAMOM PODS, LIGHTLY CRUSHED

Put the milk in a large saucepan and simmer for about 45 minutes, or until it is reduced to a thick, lumpy consistency. Stir occasionally and be careful not to let the milk burn.

When the milk has reduced, stir in the sugar, then add the almonds and cook for 2 minutes. Spread on a buttered plate and sprinkle with the crushed cardamom seeds. Serve warm, cut into diamond shapes.

SERVES 4
PREPARATION TIME: 5 MINUTES
COOKING TIME: 50 MINUTES

Sweet Lassi

300 ML/½ PINT NATURAL YOGURT
300 ML/½ PINT MILK
½ TEASPOON KEWRA WATER OR ROSE WATER
SUGAR
ICE CUBES

Place the yogurt, milk and kewra water or rose water in a liquidizer, with sugar to taste. Add some ice cubes and blend until the ice cubes have almost disappeared.

Pour into tall glasses and serve at once.

SERVES 4

PREPARATION TIME: 5 MINUTES

Salted Lassi

300 ML/½ PINT NATURAL YOGURT
300 ML/½ PINT CHILLED MILK
JUICE OF 1 LEMON
1 TEASPOON CUMIN SEEDS, ROASTED AND GROUND
½–1 TEASPOON SALT
ICE CUBES

Place the yogurt, milk, lemon juice, cumin and salt into a liquidizer. Add some ice cubes and blend briefly. Taste and add more salt if necessary, then pour into tall glasses and serve at once.

SERVES 4

PREPARATION TIME: 5 MINUTES

Index

R

S

T

Useful Addresses

Specialist Equipment and Ingredients

The Balti House Kitchen
PO Box 4401
Henley-on-Thames
Oxfordshire
RG9 1FW

The Curry Club
PO Box 7
Haslemere
Surrey
GU27 1BP

Fox's Spices Ltd
Dept GF
Masons Road
Stratford upon Avon
Warks
CV37 9NF

Balti Dishes
UK Marketing
PO Box 37
Brierley Hill
DY5 3WN

The Balti Kitchen
PO Box 385
Wolverhampton
WV2 4PD

Birmingham Balti Co
308 Telsen Centre
55 Thomas St. Aston
Birmingham
B6 4TN

Information Services

Schwartz Information
Service
Thame Road
Haddenham
Bucks HP17 8LB